11·22·78

MONEY HARD AND SOFT

MONEY HARD AND SOFT

ON THE INTERNATIONAL CURRENCY MARKETS

Brendan Brown

Foreword by
Robert Z. Aliber

A HALSTED PRESS BOOK

John Wiley & Sons
New York

First published 1978 by
THE MACMILLAN PRESS LTD
London and Basingstoke

Published in the U.S.A.
by Halsted Press, a Division
of John Wiley & Sons, Inc.

Library of Congress Cataloging in Publication Data

Brown, Brendan.
    Money hard and soft on the international currency
markets.

    "A Halsted Press book."
    Bibliography: p.
    Includes index.
    1. Foreign exchange.   2. Money.   3. Speculation.
I. Title.
HG3851.B76 1978   332.4'5   78-16929
ISBN 0-470-26466-7

To Irene Brown

Contents

List of Tables

List of Figures

Foreword

Within the last decade two developments have transformed international financial arrangements. One has been the growth of the external currency or Euro-dollar market, which began in the late 1950s and then expanded rapidly in the latter part of the 1960s. Offshore deposits denominated in the dollar, mark and Swiss franc are now larger than the domestic deposits denominated in all currencies other than the dollar. The second was the shift from the Bretton Woods system of pegged exchange rates to a system of floating exchange rates which occurred in the 1971–3 period. For the first time in more than fifty years, all the major currencies are floating. Both developments reflect the breakdown of governmental regulatory and planning mechanisms. Both changes reflect efforts of investors to increase their returns and reduce the risk to their investments.

The growth of the external currency market occurred because it became increasingly profitable to circumvent national regulations in banking – including interest rate ceilings, portfolio regulations, and reserve requirements – and taxes, including both the deposit insurance premium and withholding taxes on interest income. Interest rates on offshore deposits were almost always higher than those on domestic deposits. Banks selling offshore deposits could pay higher interest rates because their costs were lower.

Floating exchange rates were inevitable, given the inflation of the early 1970s. Investors shifted funds to avoid the losses associated with changes in Bretton Woods parities. The increased frequency of these changes reduced credibility in parities. Investors became increasingly sensitive to the impacts of changes in monetary policy and political developments on future exchange rates.

Brendan Brown provides a reasoned analysis of the institutional factors in the international financial markets which affect investors' demand for different types of money – of dollars and sterling, Swiss francs, and gold. His story is about the patterns of international payments based on the differences in transaction costs and investor confidence. He explains why the dollar is an important currency in offshore transactions and why sterling is not, and why London is an important centre for offshore transactions and Paris and New York are not. He shows why the offshore markets for deposits in dollars, German marks, and Swiss francs are extensive, and why the banks act as 'market makers' in these currencies and as brokers in other currencies. His analysis shows why there are forward markets in some currencies and not in others, and why interbank transactions are extensive in markets for Euro-dollars, Euro-marks, and Euro-Swiss francs, and not in other Euro-markets for other currencies.

In this world of competitive monies, Brown examines the policies that central banks apply to the use of their money and security markets by non-residents. Three types of policies are identified by the types of restrictions national authorities apply to international trade in securities.

Brown argues that traders and investors have a need for an international money for economic efficiency to reduce uncertainty. Gold served this need at one time, as did sterling and then the dollar. Gold had a stabilising impact on the system. The move to reduce the role of gold in the system, led by the United States with British assistance, marks a period of currency nationalism. Sterling has lost its lustre as an international money because of soft money policies. Inflationary U.S. policies threaten the international roles of the dollar.

Brown's story is rich in metaphor – he talks of dream currencies and bear squeezes, convenience rents, Royal flushes, as well as the three types of speculation. Distinctions are drawn among currency nationalism, currency protectionism, and currency mercantilism, the major countries scored on the standing of their currencies in each league.

For much too long, discussions of international finance have been on the macro and political levels. Proposals to reform the monetary system have been viewed as part of a Grand Design, and have usually ignored the behaviour of investors and the structure and operation of markets. This volume provides a new, welcome, and needed perspective on international finance.

Robert Z. Aliber

Preface

'Il faut cultiver notre jardin' is the concluding phrase of Voltaire's *Candide*. The practical interpretation of that philosophy is complex. *Money Hard and Soft* analyses the currency and euro-deposit markets from the standpoint of the operators – speculators, arbitragers and investors – who earn their livelihood there. Finance Ministers will come and go: international meetings will make blueprints for world monetary reform. The operator need not invest much time studying such plans. Foreign exchange intervention and restrictions on tradability will continue to be imposed on different currencies at different times and in different places. The fashionable arguments for interventionist policies are of less concern than their practical distortion of the groundrules of currency trading. The methods of dealing in a freely tradable international money are often inapplicable in small restricted currencies. It is my hope that this book illuminates the essential characteristics of market conditions under varying currency regimes. Which currency fits into which category is for the practitioner to re-determine continuously. The freely tradable, international currency (hard money) has an aesthetic quality. A small restricted currency (soft money) has many squalid features. Currency forms are not immutable: hard money can have soft origins. Currency evolution is the final consideration of *Money, Hard and Soft*.

It is always difficult to trace the origin of one's own thinking. Without doubt my greatest source of inspiration was Robert Aliber's teaching at the University of Chicago. It opened up a way of looking at the international money markets that I have followed ever since.

Brian Griffiths at the City University read chapters in draft form and made many helpful comments. I have benefited from discussions with Helmut Mayer and Warren McClam at the Bank for International Settlements, Rudiger Dornbusch at the Massachussets Institute of Technology and Samuel Brittan to whom I owe a special debt of gratitude.

I have drawn on sections of my articles published in *The Banker* and thank Robin Pringle for permission to do so. Christopher Story gave me permission to use sections from articles I wrote in *International Currency Review* on the subject of Chicago's International Monetary Market and I am grateful for his help.

Many insights into the workings of currency markets have been gained from colleagues in banking – in particular Guy de Froman, Kevin Pakenham and Gerhardt Tarantik. This work owes much to the assistance of Amex Bank and the American Express International Banking Corporation.

Words are unsatisfactory to express feelings and convictions. This book could neither have been conceived nor written without the partnership of my mother, Irene Brown.

Brendan Brown

List of Abbreviations

BIS	Bank for International Settlements
BSM	Buffer stock manager
C$	Canadian dollar
CD	Certificate of deposit
CME	Chicago Mercantile Exchange
Comex	New York Commodity Exchange
DM	Deutschmark
EEC	European Economic Community
Fed.	US Federal Reserve
IMF	International Monetary Fund
IMM	Chicago International Monetary Market
IRS	US Internal Revenue Service
LDC	Less developed country
LME	London Metal Exchange
OPEC	Organisation of Petroleum Exporting Countries
PSBR	Public sector borrowing requirement
Sw. fr.	Swiss franc
UK	United Kingdom
US	United States

1 Hard and Soft Money

Most of us know that US dollars are highly suitable for inclusion in a currency investment portfolio. We know equally that Italian lire should not be represented there. As the types of currency instrument and their denomination multiply, intuition is less likely to be sufficient. Should the Italian lira not be considered, even when yielding 35 per cent per annum in the euro-market? Does that gem among currencies, the Swiss franc, lose glitter when its interest rate becomes negative? Multi-tiered money presents even more complex problems for appraisal – for example which type of Belgian franc should be selected? A methodology is developed here for ranging currencies in a continuum from 'hard' to 'soft' according to their investment appeal.

'Hardness' and 'softness' are abstract qualities, as is beauty. Recognition of a currency's quality is inevitably less intuitive than of a rose's. In no way does scrutiny of a bank-note's design help. Various properties that combine to make a money hard are introduced first. Their weighting remains still an act of judgment. Our voyage in search of the meaning of hardness will take us in this book through space and time. As we alight in Hong Kong, Zurich, Chicago, Berlin 1923, London 1976 and Mexico City 1976 – to mention a few of the stopping places – the pervasiveness of the distinction between hard and soft money is revealed. The implication for macroeconomic policy, pattern of markets, euro-money centres and investment strategies unfolds.

Before the First World War the distinction commonly drawn between hard and soft currencies was simple. A hard currency was convertible into gold at a fixed exchange rate. The monetary authority in the country of issue would stand ready to buy or sell its currency for gold and maintain its gold value within a narrow range. The hard currency bloc was effectively a system of fixed exchange rate and gold was high-powered money, both domestically and internationally. To the pre-1914 world, the term 'soft' would have described the state of a currency when its link with gold was broken. In the aftermath of the US Civil War the US dollar's gold exchange value was determined freely in the market. The dollar was freely floating against other currencies and would have been described as soft.

Today it makes no sense to classify currencies according to gold convertibility. Gold was expelled from its last refuge in the international monetary system with the closing of the American gold window in August 1971. Yet hard and soft are terms heard frequently by anyone involved with currency markets.

Legends abound with instances of metamorphoses. One of the most ingenious is Jean Cocteau's adaptation of Oedipus' encounter with the Sphynx. Having first met it in the form of a beautiful young woman, he is terrified when it changes form into a monster under the same name. Though transformation of the concept behind the words hard and soft could not be the subject of a drama, it is symptomatic of the dramatic change in form of the world monetary order.

IMPORTANCE OF FREE TRADABILITY

A *sine qua non* of currency hardness is free tradability. Residents of the country of issue are permitted to buy and sell a freely tradable currency for foreign exchange, whatever their purpose, and without interference from a national control authority. The number of currencies which approximate free tradability is very small – being more or less restricted to the US dollar, Canadian dollar, Dutch guilder, Deutsche mark, Swiss franc, Hong Kong dollar and various 'oil monies', such as the Saudi riyal.

Free tradability ensures that every holder of the currency is able to obtain at the margin an equal satisfaction from it as he could obtain from other currencies. A freely traded money must survive in an open market on the basis of its qualities. By contrast a restricted currency's use grows behind the protection of restrictions. Many of its present holders would, if the threat of legal penalties were removed, switch substantially to using other monies. The investor in currencies should consider restricted tradability as *a priori* a negative factor when assessing investment appeal. Not many non-French buy Gaullois because they realise that France's state tobacco monopoly produces an inferior product sheltered by protection. The same attitude should apply to the French franc. Residents of

France are constrained to use it as money within the country.

Non-tradability does not justify total abstention by non-residents from investing in the currency. Its exchange rate behaviour may display properties that merit its inclusion in a portfolio. Convenience yield may be derivable. For example sterling is inconvertible for UK residents for other than trade transactions. Yet non-residents continue to hold significant quantities of pounds – at the end of 1976, over £6 bn. Sterling is still used to denominate some international trade and hence is demanded as transactions balances by many non-British. The pound's exchange rate has displayed at times great volatility and has attracted investors favouring high-risk investment. Sterling is fully convertible for non-residents, despite its partial inconvertibility for residents. The status of the French franc and Italian lira is similar.

An investor should however intend to give restricted currencies only a rather limited role in his portfolio. His working presumption should be that governments restrict tradability of their currency when they have strong self-interest in doing so. Their monetary management may be below standard, yet they do not want to lose seigniorage from money issue as their citizens switched to other mediums of exchange. They may be trying to adminster a low level of interest rates, despite the general market belief that the exchange rate would depreciate sharply.

DISCLOSURE OF POLICY TARGETS

Investors in general favour currencies about which they can obtain information important in forming exchange rate expectations. Often central banks of currencies that are not fully tradable are more secretive about their policy objectives. They have a guaranteed constituency to which there is no need to sell. By contrast central banks of tradable currencies know that failure to produce a prospectus of their policy on such matters as money supply, and foreign exchange intervention, would be a powerful incentive for present holders to switch to other currencies.

The Bundesbank, US Federal Reserve and Swiss National Bank all publish at regular intervals targets for monetary growth. The figures are released each week on actual monetary growth and on foreign exchange intervention. Monetary policy and aims are discussed openly and there are informed press interviews with top personnel in the central banks. By contrast money policy in restricted currency countries is shrouded typically in secrecy. Targets are set only with reluctance and, should they ever be over or undershot by wide margins, concern is not widespread in official places except in direst circumstances.

The difference between trading currencies for which full policy and statistical disclosure is made and those for which it is not is like the difference between trading a high turnover corporate equity on Wall Street compared to one on the Milan exchange where disclosure requirements are poorly developed. Unless an investor has reason to believe that he has access to privileged information, he should prefer to deal in the broadest markets where full disclosure is made. The same principle applies to currency trading as to equity trading.

The distinction between currencies for which information is disclosed and those for which it is not can be illustrated with examples.

1. A glance at any issue of the monthly *International Financial Statistics* produced by the International Monetary Fund (IMF) reveals that money supply data for Italy is typically six months out of date. In the foreign exchange markets much of the statistical data that is released eventually is treated with caution. Such defects hamper trading and, with hindsight, were one reason why the attempt to launch an Italian lira contract in Chicago's International Monetary Market was unsuccessful.

2. The UK has a tradition of secretiveness in monetary affairs. Targets were set eventually under pressure from the IMF in late 1976. They were undershot by large margins and investors who believed they were a guide to policy would have been sorely misled. Money supply and foreign exchange reserve figures are released at monthly intervals but their make-up is often questionable. Disclosure is not made of forward exchange commitments at end-month. Direct quotas restrict sometimes bank deposit creation and then monetary data becomes difficult to interpret.

SUBTLE FORMS OF NON-TRADABILITY

The right of residents to buy or sell foreign currencies is not a sufficient condition for free tradability. Other regulations may exist that restrict trading the local money. Residents of Mexico are permitted freely to deal in foreign currencies. Yet the Mexican banking system is restricted in its dealing with non-residents and financing speculative and arbitrage operations by residents. Credit is rationed and may not be extended to non-residents except to finance certain approved projects inside Mexico. Bears on the Mexican peso have no alternative but to deal in forward markets; short-selling spot pesos is not possible. Mexican banks themselves cannot arbitrage between the local peso market and the forward peso dollar market and the dollar deposit market because of high reserve requirements of the Bank of Mexico. Non-bank Mexicans in theory could arbitrage in this way, but wide spreads exist between borrowing and lending rates and the local peso market is extremely narrow. Thus restrictions on non-resident transactions in the peso market, combined with its extreme narrowness, protect peso from competition with the US dollar. During the peso crisis in the autumn and winter of 1976, 3-month interest rates in Mexico were sometimes more than 15 per cent below covered parity with the US dollar. This history demonstrates how far a currency can be protected by impediments to short-selling. If pesos could have been borrowed by arbitragers they would have operated to ensure that peso interest rates were at covered parity with the dollar. Residents and non-residents were prevented from borrowing pesos for that purpose. They could however sell pesos spot for dollars and buy pesos forward and so earn a 15 per cent superior return to holding domestic pesos deposits for the same risk. That this did not occur to a great extent, demonstrated the extent to which domestic pesos are held for convenience return from the saving of transaction costs. At the margin the convenience yield must have equalled the un-exploited arbitrage margin.

In conclusion no restrictions must prevent short-selling the currency if the existence of large shortfalls of domestic interest rates from covered parity with dollars is to be precluded. Shortfalls indicate that the currency is uncompetitive with dollars except for those deriving some form of convenience return. Anyone looking simply for risk exposure in the restricted currency would do best taking a forward position. A positive factor for currency investment appeal must be access to domestic money and credit market for arbitragers and speculators without commercial roots in the country. They derive no convenience yield that could justify a lower purely monetary rate of return. They are the Flying Dutchmen of the world of international finance.

BLACK MARKETS

Professor Aliber attributed part of the drama of international finance to circumventing national regulations. No serious student of the subject should be unaware of a wartime fable of Marcel Aymé's – the *Life Ration*. A scheme for rationing the existence of 'useless' elements in the population – retired people, intellectuals and rentiers – was introduced. Coupons were issued entitling the unfortunates to between one and six days a week. Within a few months some people were found to be living as much as sixty days a month. The clue to the mystery was the development of a black market in time coupons. The rationing system was abolished.

Regulations which restrict currency tradability have a similar effect. Black market activity can always be identified in some form. Marcel Aymé could be accused of over-estimating the sophistication of official response.

Examples of black market ('parallel' market rates) are given in Table 1.1. There the discount of the black market below official quote varied from zero for the Italian lira to 67 per cent for the Czech croner. What significance, if any, can be attached to the size of discount?

Although the black-market quote is in some sense a 'free' market quote, it does not normally represent what the currency's rate of exchange would be if it became freely tradable in and outside the country of issue. A major determinant of the deepness of black-market discount is the ease of arbitrage between the black market and the official market.

All the countries listed in Table 1.1 except the UK ban the import of their own bank-notes. Thus lire sold on the black market have to be smuggled back into Italy or sold to tourists who are permitted to enter with limited quantities. Black-market dealers in lira, whether in Switzerland or New York, have to in the main find buyers who will either risk smuggling them into Italy and launder them there for goods and foreign exchange or tourists who will risk exceeding their allowances to cheapen their Italian vacations. Severe penalties for smuggling and high enforcement levels make for larger black-market discounts. The Czech croner discount is significant in this regard. Smugglers of croners into Czechoslovakia need a large incentive to justify their operation.

Imports of sterling bank-notes in the UK are unlimited, despite the pound not being freely tradable. Thus dealers in sterling outside

TABLE 1.1   Black-market exchange rates

	Official Rate	Black Rate
Algerian Dinar	4·12	8·33
Bangladesh Taks	15·62	40·00
Czechoslovakian Croner	9·97	25·90
Indian Rupee	8·84	10·00
S. African Rand (a)	1·10	0·80
Turkish Lira	16·30	20·00
Italian Lira	885·50	877·10ʹ
British Pound (a)	1·7183	1·5981

Notes:
1 Source. International Reports Inc. Statistical Market Letter. 10 June 1977.
2 (a) signifies rate expressed as US dollars per foreign currency unit.
3 All rates are 'bid' rates.
4 Rates are as quoted in the New York 'parallel' markets.

the UK can buy smuggled sterling and ship it back to the credit of a non-resident sterling account in the UK; then it is exchanged legitimately in the foreign-exchange market. Discounts in the sterling black market reflect therefore only the cost of transporting notes. Discounts are narrower on large deals because the shipping costs per unit value decrease. For the other currencies listed, where re-import of notes is not possible, discounts widen for larger transactions. The dealer risks holding a large inventory of notes, and suffering an adverse rate movement, before he can dispose of them; so he quotes a lower bid rate.

For given impediments to arbitrage, variation in the black-market discount is indicative of changing excess supply of the currency at its present official exchange rate. In March 1976, when fear was widespread of a Communist general election victory in Italy, the discount on black-market lire deepened to as much as 15 per cent. Table 1.1 illustrates that by June 1977 the discount had fallen to zero. Enforcement powers of the Italian authorities had not increased notably during the interval. The narrowing of the discount must be attributed to a reduction of net excess supply of lire at the June official exchange rate, indicating a firmer basis for that parity than a year previously. The Bank of Italy is indeed sensitive to movements of the black-market rate as an indicator of likely pressures on the currency. Widening discounts tend to indicate a greater outflow of smuggled money and consequent eventual diversion of lire purchases from the official market. Currency traders should equally treat with respect black-market quotations.

BID-OFFER SPREADS IN BANK-NOTE MARKETS

Not only are the bank-note (black market) rates of non-freely tradable currencies typically below official rates, but bid-offer rates quoted by dealers are also wider than on freely tradable currency bank-notes. The relation is demonstrated in Table 1.2. Spreads on restricted currencies, such as those of South Africa, Czechoslovakia and Italy, are much wider than for the US dollar, West German mark or Dutch guilder.

TABLE 1.2   Bid-offer bank-note quotes, Basel, June 1977

Australia	2·60–2·90
US $	2·45–2·55
DM	104·25–106·75
Austria	14·75–15·05
French franc	49·25–51·25
Pound sterling	4·15–4·45
E. Germany	24–28
Czech	9·75–11·75
S. Africa	2·05–2·45
Israel	0·25–0·35
Portugal	5·75–7·25
Holland	100·25–102·25
Italy	27·75–29·75
Egypt	3·35–3·85

Notes: Rates are against Swiss franc, for volume of less than Sw. fr. 50,000.

The source of differing spreads is to be found in the cost of market-making. The market-maker in bank-notes of freely convertible currencies bears less risk and hence can charge a lower bid-offer spread. At the end of a day's business, if he finds himself with a large excess inventory of notes, he can ship these to banks in the country of issue and exchange for Swiss francs at the highly competitive telegraphic transfer rate. Interest loss and exchange risk will be minimal. By contrast, the bank-note market-maker in restricted currencies has usually no such option because import of bank-notes is prohibited. A secondary explanation is that markets are much narrower in bank-notes of restricted currencies due to the limitations on their free flow.

DREAM CURRENCIES

Euromoney (August 1976) carried a report about portfolio management by Swiss banks. Clients are often asked what currency they dream in. Their investment portfolio performance is reported in the dream currency. One Hungarian-born refugee living in Latin America dreamt, it emerged, in deutschmarks because of the dominant Germanic influence in the Hungary of his youth.

Very few currencies have transcended the confines of its nation state to be so used as a unit of account between non-residents who have no obvious connection with the country of issue. Such currencies shall be termed here 'dream currencies'. They include the Swiss franc, West German mark and US dollar.

QUALITIES OF DREAM CURRENCIES

Some monies attain dream status because of the importance of the issuer in the world economy, others because of the excellence of their management. The US dollar's widespread use outside the US is undoubtedly attributable to that country's prime role. Many of the goods in world trade have prices fixed in US dollars. If the dollar depreciated sharply, their dollar price would be slow to change and would often not adjust by the full extent of the depreciation. US purchasing power would have been cut in terms of other currencies and it is a major component of demand for many products. Thus in holding dollars (or borrowing dollars) the transactor has less reason to be concerned about relative exchange rate adjustments than for any other currency. The variability of the real purchasing power of his dollar balances should be small.

The West German mark, and more particularly the Swiss franc, have earned their dream status due to the high quality of their management. Monetary authorities in both Switzerland and West Germany have placed great emphasis on price stability. Inflation (in terms of West German marks or Swiss francs) and its variability has been among the lowest in the world. Therefore many transactors outside Switzerland and Germany have chosen these currencies as unit of account to denominate borrowing and lending. They hope to minimise the uncertainty of inflation and its impact on the real value of their debts and assets.

RANKING DREAM CURRENCIES

What are the symptoms of a dream currency? One is its frequent selection as a unit of account to denominate portfolio valuations by Swiss banks. The importance of the choice of currency in which to measure portfolio performance should not be underestimated. Only in a world of certainty would the choice be immaterial. Otherwise a portfolio's risk changes according to the measuring rod. If Swiss francs are chosen as the numeraire, Swiss franc securities will gain weight in the portfolio, so decreasing risk: and similarly for other currencies.

The growth of euro-bond, foreign bond, and euro-deposit markets in a given currency are symptomatic of it having joined the 'dream set'. The markets are used widely by non-residents of the country of issue for the purpose of denominating loan transactions. Markets in the Swiss franc, US dollar and West German mark are predominant (see Tables 1.3 and 1.4).

Changing proportions of each of the Swiss franc, US dollar and West German mark in the total are indicative of their changing

TABLE 1.3   Size of euro-deposit markets by currency $m

	US $s	DMs	Sw. frs	£s	Guilders	French francs
1968	26870	3010	2290	800	250	230
1969	46200	4640	4030	810	350	210
1970	58700	8080	5720	940	550	420
1971	70750	14630	7760	2110	860	440
1972	96730	19540	8810	2210	1360	1080
1973	131380	32020	17160	4790	2260	2130
1974	156430	34380	18290	3590	2760	2270
1975	189470	39940	15290	3140	3550	3350
1976	230040	47230	15880	3980	3530	3220

Notes:
1 Source: *B.I.S. Annual Report*, 1977.
2 Figures include interbank positions.

TABLE 1.4 International bond issues by currency of denomination 1974–6 $m

	US $s	DMs	Sw. frs
1974	6670	640	990
1975	11570	2890	3370
1976	20000	2780	5220

Notes:
1 Only the Swiss franc figures includes private placements.
2 US dollar issues include the 'yankee bond' market in New York.
3 Source: Morgan Guaranty.

popularity as units of account. For example the popularity of the West German mark could be deemed to have decreased from 1974 to 1976. In the second quarter of 1977 the proportion of Swiss franc issues slumped dramatically to 5 per cent from 15 per cent in the same period during the previous year. Following the shattering revelation in April 1977 about Credit Suisse's Chiasso branch, where over $1 billion were believed lost, the immediate outlook for the Swiss franc became uncertain. Both borrowers and lenders shy away from units of account whose movement is potentially volatile. The decrease in Swiss franc issues should not be interpreted either as indicating a market belief that the franc would strengthen or weaken by more than its interest rate differential with other currencies.

Changing popularity of units of account is also a feature of domestic capital markets. Increased volatility of inflation rates has been responsible for a tendency for the maturity of bond issues to shorten. Neither borrowers nor lenders wish to assume the risk of large fluctuations in the real value of their mutual obligations. Short-term debt instruments are substituted for long.

CHANGING CURRENCY POPULARITY

Tables 1.3 and 1.4 demonstrate that swings in currency popularity can be marked. Yet a currency's exchange rate may be unaffected by them, if both lenders and borrowers show equal propensity to shift to other units of account. Suppose they both wish to reduce exposure to Swiss francs by $1 billion and switch that amount to dollar denomination. As investors sell Swiss franc bonds and buy dollar bonds, borrowers simultaneously buy back their Swiss franc bonds and issue US dollar bonds. Nothing in the process would generate a change in the Swiss franc – US dollar exchange rate.

A desired switch in unit of account in the euro-money markets can have wider implications. Euro-banking operations depend on ultimate access to a pool of high-powered money in a domestic banking system. High-powered money is a debt obligation of governments which is unlikely to act in sympathy with market sentiment. In the example of currency taste shifting to dollars from francs, the Swiss government would be unlikely to follow market fashion by reducing high-powered franc money supply and borrowing instead short-term euro-dollars. The asymmetry so introduced would induce an exchange-rate depreciation.

The notion of symmetrical changes in taste of borrowers and lenders having no effect on the exchange rate cannot apply to currencies with restricted tradability. Normally non-residents are not able to borrow these yet they can hold them freely for investment purposes. If sentiment towards the currency changes because of increased volatility, depreciation pressure will result as investment demand decreases. Unlike freely tradable currencies, there is no balancing force of borrowers switching to another denomination to offset that of investors withdrawing.

MINOR EURO-MARKETS

Euro-markets exist in denominations outside the 'big three' – the West German mark, US dollar and Swiss franc. They are based on a combination of convenience factors rather than on their popularity as a unit of account. For example a small Canadian dollar deposit market has grown in London in recent years. Corporations based in Europe want to deal in Canadian dollars before Canada wakes up each day.

Language problems should not be under-rated as a basis for euro-market growth: many corporations feel more comfortable borrowing guilders from a London bank than negotiating a similar transaction in the Netherlands. The euro-guilder and euro-Canadian dollar markets could both be termed 'convenience euro-markets'.

The importance of tax factors as a basis for euro-growth is demonstrated by the birth of the Hong Kong dollar as a denominator in the euro-bond market in the spring of 1977. A loophole in the Hong Kong tax code excludes issues subscribed for foreign currencies from Hong Kong withholding tax. Such issues are therefore very popular in Hong Kong itself. To date euro-Hong Kong dollar bonds have been sold almost entirely to Hong Kong residents and the market's growth signifies in no way the assumption of dream qualities by the Hong Kong dollar.

Small euro-deposit markets exist in some currencies which have restricted tradability in their domestic form. These euro-markets may be described as 'free' compared to the protected domestic market. Their growth is attributed in part to this 'freedom', and is analysed in a later section (p. 21).

SMALL AND LARGE

Between January 1976 and June 1977 the one-month euro-guilder deposit rate rose from 5 per cent to over 15 per cent by July 1976 and fell back to below 3 per cent by June 1977. Over the same time interval three-month euro-dollar deposit rates traded within a range of 5 per cent to 6 per cent and euro-deutsch mark three-month rates from $3\frac{3}{4}$ to 5 per cent. Yet inflation differentials expected between US, Germany and Netherlands could never have exceeded 4 per cent over the relevant time intervals. This recent case history of the euro-markets demonstrates that the laws of motion of interest rates in small and large currencies are very different.

LAWS OF INTEREST MOTION FOR FREELY TRADABLE CURRENCIES

Proposition 1: On small currencies, short-term interest rates plus expected appreciation against the US dollar tends to equal the same maturity euro-dollar rate.

Proposition 2: On large currencies, interest rates – short and long – are dominated by domestic inflation expectations. If the exchange rate is not expected to move consistently with differential inflation, then proposition 1 does not apply here.

Proposition 3: The smaller the currency, the greater will be the volatility of interest rates engendered by spot exchange-market intervention.

LAWS EXPLAINED

Hedgers of foreign currency denominated trade invoices are a major source of forward exchange business. Small currencies are issued normally by very open economies for which international trade accounts for a high proportion of GNP. The proportion of outstanding forward exchange positions to the size of the domestic credit market is thus larger for small currencies. Further the proportion of speculative positions to hedging positions does not alter appreciably with the size of the forward market. Hence the ratio of speculative positions to the size of credit markets increases as the currency becomes smaller.

Arbitrage ensures that domestic interest rates are at covered parity with US dollar interest rates. It is often queried though how far forward rates of exchange reflect expected exchange rates. Equivalently, how reliable are cross-currency interest rate differentials as estimates of exchange rate expectations.

Suppose the market revises down its expectations of future spot exchange rates of a currency and that the forward exchange rate adjusts to remain equal to the expected level. Covered interest arbitrage would result. Arbitrage demand for funds represents an extra demand in the domestic credit market. If the credit market is narrow relative to the forward exchange market, interest rates will adjust up by almost the full amount of the initial arbitrage margin and the forward rate will remain nearly equal to the expected spot rate. That is the small currency case. For large currencies the forward market is narrow relative to the domestic credit market, interest rates hardly respond to exchange market pressure and substantial divergencies occur between forward rates and exchange rate expectations.

Two further considerations accentuate the relative exchange market sensitivity of small currency interest rates:

1. Resident commitment is less to the local unit of account. Sophisticate investors in small open economies tend to measure at least part of their wealth in one of the three dream currencies – US dollars, West German marks and Swiss francs. A higher proportion of investors in local small currency denominated assets stand ready to switch to their dream currency when the former is under suspicion. The elasticity of supply of speculative funds is high with respect to a divergence of the interest rate differential between the

small currency and US dollar from the expected relative exchange
rate movement.

2. Leads and lags in trade payments in response to exchange rate
expectations tend to be a property of small currencies. Leads and
lags can engender net credit demands that are of significance relative
to the domestic credit market, especially in small open economies.

LEADS AND LAGS

Leads and lags are an important vehicle of speculation in currencies
with restricted tradability. Many other forms of taking a view on the
currency's prospects are prevented. Less generally understood is the
particular attraction of leading and lagging in a small currency.
The guilder is taken here as an illustration.

Suppose the guilder is expected to depreciate sharply, say over
the next three months. For reasons discussed already (excluding
leads and lags) guilder interest rates will have risen sharply because
the pull of gravity from domestic inflation expectations is small. A
US resident importer from the Netherlands could take a short
position in the guilder without incurring the now much increased
interest cost. He delays making payment against his guilder invoices
hoping to purchase guilders at a cheaper rate. It is true that he can,
even in more stable times, take a short position against the guilder
by delaying payment but the incentive to do so is greatest during a
crisis period when the interest saving is greatest. The guilder credit
demand so generated adds to the upward pressure on interest rates
during the currency crisis.

The same type of leads and lags opportunities do not present
themselves between 'heavy weight' currencies. Were an imminent
depreciation of the US dollar against the West German mark
expected, the interest rate differential between US dollars and West
German marks would be little changed. No special incentive would
be created for leading and lagging compared to more normal times.

Only in restricted currency markets does it make sense for a local
resident to short-sell the local currency by accelerating payment of
foreign currency invoices. Otherwise a more profitable strategy is to
borrow locally, switch the proceeds into dollars and have the benefit
of interest earnings on those dollars. The reader will find, as he
works through other examples of leading and lagging in freely

tradable currencies, that only one type would rationally be adopted. Foreigners would delay payment of invoices denominated in small currencies.

SMALL CURRENCY SPECULATION

The astronomical analogy used in demonstrating the laws of interest rate motion may usefully be extended. The force of gravity of non-speculative credit transactions on interest rates is much greater for large currencies than small and pulls rates away from the level that reflects expected exchange rate movement.

The rewards of speculating in large currencies are potentially larger than in small. Divergencies of interest rate differentials from exchange rate expectations are the juice of currency trading.

In all credit markets, whether denominated in small or large currencies, the proportion of trade related transactions – and hence speculative positions – decreases for longer maturities. Divergencies of long-term interest rates from long-term exchange rate expectations are therefore greater than for short. The rewards to currency trading are greater the further out we move along the maturity structure. The pull of gravity of domestic inflation expectations is greater in the long-term credit markets than the short.

Our third law of interest rate motion asserts that the smaller the currency, the greater will be the volatility of interest rates engendered by spot exchange market intervention. The law can be deduced from the first two. If a small currency central bank resists a movement – in either direction – of its spot exchange rate, an immediate change in its forward discount/premium will occur. Presumably expectations about the future level of the exchange rate are mainly unaltered, so that the forward rate is at first hardly affected. A temporary covered interest arbitrage opportunity is so created which in the small currency case is eliminated primarily by a movement of the interest rate rather than forward exchange rate. In a large currency it is true that spot intervention gives rise similarly to a divergence of interest rates from covered parity, but here the arbitrage gap is closed by an adjustment of the forward exchange rate away from its assumed unaltered expected future spot rate. So in large currencies intervention to 'stabilise' the spot exchange rate tends to have the same influence on the forward exchange rate, the two being tied together by a steady domestic interest rate.

In small currencies, the interest rate link between spot and forward exchange rates is very elastic. Stabilisation of the spot rate has little spillover on the forward exchange market and, if times are uncertain, volatility of the latter will remain. The phenomenon of greater variability of currency forward rates than spot rates in small currencies, such as the guilder and Belgian franc, is widely acknowledged by traders.

SMALL CURRENCY COMPLEX

Central banks of small currencies are often intensely aware of the critical exposure of their domestic interest rate structure to external influences. Some accept the consequential interest rate volatility as a fact of economic life and take no action to combat it. Others–the 'currency nationalists' who are analysed in Chapter 5–battle against their natural misfortune using a variety of weapons. They include the institution of dual exchange markets and other systems of exchange restriction. Their common feature is the limiting of arbitrage flows between the domestic credit and forward exchange market.

The choice between nationalism and internationalism does not have to be forced in this form by central banks of large currencies. They have been blessed with a natural shelter from the international economy.

DANGER OF SMALL CURRENCY OVERKILL

A central bank must be very wary about effecting measures to reduce the natural hypersensitivity of a small credit market to external influences. It risks spoiling the market for its currency. This proposition can be illustrated with two examples.

1. Dual exchange markets. Their institution, by dividing foreign exchange transactions between two markets, makes each narrower than a unified one would be. Bid-ask spreads are thus widened in foreign exchange dealings involving the small currency and it becomes less attractive for speculators and arbitragers to deal in.

The failure of the Belgian franc to excite international investment interest is ascribed widely to the two-tier division of its market into convertible and financier categories and the narrowness of each.

2. Another method of reducing interest rate volatility is to abstain from spot exchange market intervention. But then, unless monetary policy is well harmonised with larger countries, the spot exchange rate will assume a motion independent of larger currencies. Unless that motion is in itself attractive – as is the case with the Swiss franc – independence is not a quality sought by holders of small currencies who are typically local residents of the country of issue. Independence widens the bid-ask spread on foreign exchange deals and local traders, who are significant potential holders of the small currency, would be likely to switch to making more use of foreign currency deposits. In this way the higher exchange transaction costs may be avoided.

MONEY MANAGEMENT BURDEN

Small currency management is no light burden. The exceptionally talented central bank can foster the growth of its small currency into a world major. The Swiss have accomplished this by a long reputation of excellent management so that the franc has become one of the dream currencies. The total Swiss franc denominated credit market is many times greater than its domestic submarket in which Swiss residents borrow and lend. The franc has thus earned the interest rate independence bestowed on currencies of large economies.

Less talented central banks have chosen in general to tie their currencies to larger groupings, like the European 'Snake'. They hope thereby to narrow dealing costs in their foreign exchange market and increase demand for their issue. Management of a tied currency is not easy. If interest rate volatility is to be avoided, a monetary policy must be followed that is consistent with the fixed exchange rate and is credible on the markets. The chance of forward exchange rates fluctuating widely is reduced as expectations of continued currency stability prevail.

MONIES IN COMPETITION

If a currency is freely tradable, its expected real rate of interest must tend to equal that on other freely tradable currencies (like the US dollar) after adjustment is made for risk. The relation is complicated sometimes by convenience return considerations. Professor Aliber found that the real interest rate on US dollar bills tended to be smaller than on Canadian dollar bills. This was despite both currencies being freely tradable. His explanation of the discrepancy was that the US dollar is a more popular currency than the Canadian dollar and that the margin holders of Canadian dollars must earn a premium as inducement. An asymmetry between popularity for lenders and borrowers is implied. If the Canadian dollar was equally unpopular with both borrowers and lenders at the margin, its expected real interest rate would have to equal that of the US dollar. The inequality discovered by Professor Aliber indicates that borrowers of Canadian dollars must, at the margin, receive a convenience yield from choosing that denomination in preference to US dollars. Borrowers' convenience yield is discussed further in Chapter 3.

In certain Latin American countries expected real interest rates in the local money and credit markets have been substantially greater than on US dollars, despite the currency having restricted tradability. Inflation rates are volatile and real rates of return very volatile. The superiority of the local real interest rate to the dollar rate is most likely not sufficient to offset the extreme unpopularity of the currency as a unit of account for many investors. If free tradability were granted, interest rates on the local currency would rise and domestic borrowers as well as lenders would switch in part to foreign currencies.

INSTITUTIONAL IMPEDIMENTS TO TRADE

Even where no government restrictions impede competition in monies institutional characteristics may do so. Examples include:

1. *Poorly developed domestic money market*

Where the domestic credit or money markets are poorly developed the speculative and arbitrage operations that enforce competitiveness between local and foreign real interest rates are slower and more costly. The domestic Swiss franc market is an example of one without either Treasury Bill or interbank trading. A certain degree of insulation would surround domestic Swiss interest rates even without the added control laws of the Swiss National Bank.

2. *Different trading dates*

In the euro-deposit and foreign exchange markets most trading is for 'value dates' at least two days in the future. What is termed a spot exchange transaction is for settlement in two business days' time. Narrow markets exist typically for 'tomorrow-next (T/N)' and 'spot-next (S/N)' transactions. Consider a market-maker in Swiss francs who quoted the following rates against the US dollar on 6 July 1977:

Spot	2·4235–40
1 month	48/45
3 month	140/135
6 month	200/192
1 year	350/340
T/N	3/5
S/N	3/5

The spot rate of 2·4235 would be for settlement on 8 July, T/N is the discount for settlement on 7 July compared to 8 July and the 7 July rate is 2·4238–45. Similarly the 9 July settlement rate is 2·4230– 37. It is exceptional to find exchange markets for immediate settlement today and tomorrow markets (T/N) do not exist normally after midday. Thus overnight domestic interest rates are insulated largely from arbitrage or speculative pressures arising from the foreign exchange markets. Practice in the euro-markets follows that in the foreign exchange markets, and overnight markets of any depth exist (for today and tomorrow) only in the US dollar. Euro-deposit markets other than in the US dollar, West German mark and Swiss franc are in the main a creature of various 'swap transactions' in foreign exchange to be discussed further in Chapter 2 (p. 46). It would therefore be unusual for trading dates in euro-deposits for other than the three dream currencies to be different from those in the foreign exchange market. The lack of overnight trading in West German marks and Swiss francs, and a minor amount in sterling, is due to technical clearing considerations which is beyond the scope of the present book to describe.

In short competition between monies for very short maturities (1–2 days) is simply not possible in most cases because of the technical organisation of the euro-deposit and foreign exchange markets. Overnight West German mark interest rates in Frankfurt for example are effectively insulated from international pressures.

PARALLEL DEPOSIT MARKETS

During the heady days of the 1976 sterling crisis, three-month euro-sterling rates in Paris were sometimes as much as 5 per cent greater than domestic sterling. In more normal times it is not unusual for euro-pound interest rates to be 2–3 per cent greater than domestic pound rates.

Euro-pound rates are often greater than domestic pound rates because there is more competition between euro-pounds and euro-dollars than between domestic pounds and euro-dollars. Euro-pounds are freely tradable and may be borrowed and lent without restriction for foreign exchange speculation. The expected real interest rate on euro-pounds tends therefore to equal that on euro-dollars, adjusted for risk factors.

The analysis has so far been couched in terms of pounds, but applies equally to any euro-market in a currency whose tradability is restricted. Another example is the relationship between euro-French franc and domestic French franc rates of interest.

The relation between euro- and domestic rates for restricted monies is analogous to that between the exchange rates in the parallel ('black') market and official market. The interest rate differential is in part a function of the ease of arbitrage between the parallel (euro-) deposit market and the domestic (official) one. Further, for a given degree of enforcement of regulations impeding arbitrage between the two markets, movements in the interest rate differential are indicative of unsatisfied net credit demand at the official (domestic) market interest rate. When in October 1976 the euro-pound domestic pound interest rate differential widened suddenly, the cause was a surge of demand for borrowing pounds to sell for dollars. Yet exchange regulations prevented access to the domestic pound market for this purpose. Demand for pounds was deflected to the euro-market.

It has been shown already that the black market exchange rate should not be equated to that which would prevail if all restrictions were abolished. Similarly the euro- (parallel, black) rate on sterling or French franc deposits does not in general equal what the interest rate would be in the domestic market if restrictions there were abolished. The new interest rate would depend on the comparative popularity of the currency for both borrowers and lenders who would be primarily domestic residents now freed to exercise currency choice.

The distinction between the euro-interest rate and the domestic interest rate which would be established if currency restrictions were removed is illustrated by recent Italian financial history. During the 1976 lira crisis domestic interest rates in Italy were as much as 15 per cent below covered parity with euro-dollars. The large differential reflected substantial unsatisfied demand for domestic lira credits by potential short-sellers of the currency. They resorted to selling lire in the forward markets, or to borrowing euro-lire. By the summer of 1977 the differential had declined to zero. The relation of the level of interest rates in an unrestricted lira credit market to those ruling then would be difficult to assess.

INVESTMENT IN PARALLEL DEPOSIT MARKETS

Attention has been drawn to the greater competitiveness of euro- than domestic markets in currencies with restricted tradability. Could such 'parallel' deposit markets ever become a popular form of investment with non-residents of the country of currency issue? The answer is in practice negative.

Firstly bid-offer spreads in parallel deposit markets tend to be wide. Their artificial separation from the domestic market causes them to suffer from narrowness. Transaction costs are an important consideration to many operators in choosing currency investments.

Secondly though the development of a parallel market provides a more attractive form in which to hold the restricted currency, its denomination in the same unit account as the domestic market remains fundamental. The exchange rate is likely to be volatile and central bank monetary policy secretive. Assuming the features mentioned are as unpopular with would-be borrowers as lenders, growth of the euro-market must be limited. Euro-growth is heavily dependent on the currency being freely tradable in both domestic and euro-form.

SWISS SHANGRI-LA

The motive of the Swiss authorities in restricting arbitrage flows from the euro-franc market into the domestic has been the reverse of that of the UK or France in applying restrictions in the opposite direction. The Swiss controls have had the typical effect of maintaining domestic interest rates at a higher level than in the euro-market. Many inflation-weary investors all over the world have in recent years purchased Swiss franc deposits as the ultimate hedge. By effectively channelling such flows outside Switzerland the authorities have insulated domestic real interest rates obtainable by the Swiss at a high real level and have protected them from the ravages of the world inflationary storm. Foreigners seeking shelter can at most penetrate the outer courtyard of the form of the external franc market. A barrage of negative interest taxes and withholding taxes keeps the inner garden of the franc money market impenetrable. Those who found a devious pathway through the gates of the Credit Suisse branch at Chiasso were eventually rejected badly bruised.

CALCULATION IN SPECULATION

At various stages in this book techniques of currency trading and investment are discussed at some depth. As a group currency traders and investors have an importance in the macroeconomy that has often been ignored. In a free currency market, where no central bank intervention occurs, the role of the speculator is essential to a smooth international flow of both capital and goods.

MODEL ECONOMY

As a generalisation two types of goods are produced and consumed in an economy – tradable and non-tradable. The latter do not enter into international trade and include such examples as buildings and haircuts. Most economies are price-takers in the world market for traded goods. The impact effect of an exchange rate change is therefore to alter proportionately the relative price of traded to non-traded goods in the domestic economy. Relative price change generates in turn trade balance effects. An exchange rate depreciation, by raising the relative price of traded goods, induces domestic producers to switch to producing traded goods and consumers to buying non-traded ones. The net effect is an increased trade surplus.

In the long run exchange rates tend to move consistently with differential inflation rates. Deviations from this purchasing power parity relation – some temporary, some permanent – can occur and can be considered as real exchange rate changes. They are caused by either currency speculators anticipating capital movements or changes in relative productivity in the traded and non-traded goods sectors or by changes in domestic taste for the two types of goods.

THREE SPECULATIVE RESPONSES

To examine how the speculator calculates three exogenous shocks to the international payments structure of an economy are considered. The nature of real exchange rates is further illuminated.

1. *Shift in currency taste*

Suppose a large net foreign demand arises for assets denominated in a given currency, for example Swiss francs. The cause is assumed to be a shift in investor taste for that particular money brand. In the aftermath of the 1971 collapse of the Bretton Woods system and the 1973 quadrupling of the oil price, a sudden net increase in demand for Swiss francs as a refuge doubtless occurred.

In the long run the net demand for francs must be accomodated by an equal offsetting Swiss trade or long-term capital account deficit. Patterns of trade and long-term capital-flows are slow to change and in the short run the new net investment demand is accommodated by speculators. They short-sell Swiss francs to investors. Speculators have assumed two main forms in the Swiss example. Firstly corporations and banks have borrowed Swiss francs to finance acquisition of non-franc assets thus running a short position in the currency. Secondly the foreign bond market in Swiss francs has boomed in Switzerland since 1974 and been a vehicle for assuming short positions. Borrowing there has been by non-Swiss and on condition that proceeds are converted immediately for foreign currency at the Swiss National Bank.

Some of the increased borrowing of Swiss francs is doubtless by those who have been attracted to it as a unit of account or as a dream currency. That part is deducted from increased investor demand for Swiss francs to arrive at the total new net investors' demand.

The speculators who short-sell francs to the investor intend to close their exposure when a deficit in Switzerland's basic balance of payments materialises eventually. Swiss francs are generated via the basic deficit for the speculators to purchase in order to repay their loans.

The speculator must calculate the spot exchange rate which makes the whole risk operation worthwhile. First he estimates the net investment demand overhanging the market. In the long-run that net demand must be accommodated by an equal cumulative basic balance of payments deficit. He determines next the immediate appreciation of the franc needed to generate a trade deficit which, together with estimated long-term capital flows, equals the required basic deficit. Under certain common assumptions the immediate appreciation equals the new net demand divided by the Swiss money supply. Long-term capital flows are, as a first approximation, unresponsive to exchange rate changes.

Adam Smith wrote 'It is not from the benevolence of the butcher, the brewer, or the baker that we expect our dinner, but from their regard to their own interest.' Nor should altruism be expected from currency speculators. In return for taking their short position they expect to earn a risk premium. The speculator shorting the Swiss franc against the US dollar must expect the dollar equivalent cost of borrowing Swiss francs to be less than the dollar interest rate. That inequality holds if the interest rate differential between dollars and francs is less than the realized appreciation of the franc against the dollar. The rate of appreciation should be less than the differential inflation rate between the US and Switzerland because the exchange rate overshot its 'purchasing power parity level' in response to net demand for Swiss francs. Once the basic deficit has been generated the exchange rate will have returned to the path consistent with differential inflation between the two countries. The initial real appreciation of the franc is so followed by a gradual real depreciation back to its initial real level.

Sometimes the exchange rate will appreciate initially by more than is necessary to generate the required trade deficit. In a large currency, as has been demonstrated, interest rates are pulled heavily by the gravity of domestic inflation expectations. If the speculator is to be tempted to short-sell, his risk premium must be earned by the currency appreciating 'too much' at first, 'too large' a trade deficit being generated. In consequence the exchange rate follows a steeper path back to the main highway of purchasing power parity. In a small currency overshooting of the exchange rate is less as greater interest rate flexibility provides part of the speculator's returns.

2. *Natural resource discovery*

Gold mines, oil field, uranium deposit discoveries are the chips from life's roulette wheel that can change the destiny of nations. It is rarely interesting to use collectivist terminology. A nation is a collection of many different individuals in multitudinous roles. Who, in which role, gains most?

Consider the example of a country such as the UK that discovers oil fields within its territory. Over many years they are expected to generate significant net export earnings equal to the rental element in total oil receipts. Ignoring the possibility of foreign exchange market intervention the sterling exchange rate would be likely to depreciate by less against the US dollar than differential inflation between the UK and USA would justify. The consequential real appreciation of sterling by causing an increase in the relative price of non-traded goods in the UK, generates a non-oil trade deficit, offsetting the surplus on trade account. The real exchange rate continues to appreciate as oil receipts grow typically from a modest start to significant sums later. Hence a time pattern of growing non-oil deficits is required. Interest rates, both long and short, are likely to be considerably lower than inflation as the exchange rate is expected to depreciate by less than differential inflation. The degree of negativity of real interest rates will depend on the size of currency, smaller credit markets being more exchange market sensitive.

3. *Improved domestic investment opportunity*

Suppose that the threat of government price and profit controls were removed in France. A shift upwards would occur in the expected real return to capital invested in French projects. Non-residents would wish to increase direct investment in France and a potential net capital inflow would overhang the franc exchange market. Again, assuming no intervention by the central bank, what adjustments occur?

This time the desired capital inflow creates its own trade deficit and the services of the currency's speculator are not required. Corresponding to the inflow on capital account is a capital goods inflow through the current account of the balance of payments. Increased direct investment takes the form of importation of capital equipment to combine with French labour and land to obtain the now surer rates of return.

WINDFALL GAINS NOT RANDOM

Who gains from the three types of disturbances just described is not random. The gains from the first type – increased net demand for the currency as a denominator – are those who held it when the shift in popularity occurred. They benefit from its immediate appreciation.

Landowners gain more than anyone from the second type of disturbance. Real estate is the purest non-traded good and tends to increase in price proportionately with an index of non-traded goods prices. Yet the interest rate is less than the domestic inflation rate expected and certainly less than the rate of inflation of non-traded goods. Thus an immediate increase in value occurs for buildings and land to equate the expected rate of return with that on other assets and the rate of interest.

The gainer from the third type of disturbance is the holder of equities in domestic enterprises. The improvement in investment prospects causes an immediate gain in equity values. The expected rate of return on equities is thus equated to the unchanged domestic rate of interest determined competitively in the world markets. This conclusion is dependent on the domestic currency being freely tradable.

In sum the gainer is the person who made commitment of venture capital to the object which has been favoured by fortune. The investor in Swiss francs gains from events that cause a sudden shift in demand for them – whether an OPEC or world inflation shock or the appointment of a talented team to run the central bank. The person who owns land in a country gains from a natural resource discovery there. Land is the most immovable of assets and investors in it stake most in fortunes that are specific to that particular state. The equity holder in local enterprises has most at stake in changes in industrial investment climate.

NEUTRAL SHIFTS IN CURRENCY TASTE

Speculative response is not always required to bridge a shift in currency taste. Imagine both residents and non-residents wishing to decrease their exposure in guilders by 10 per cent in real terms. Further the Dutch Central Bank pursues an unchanged money supply target. Equilibrium can be restored by a 10 per cent increase in the domestic price level and a 10 per cent depreciation of the exchange rate. No currency flows across international boundaries for the necessary adjustment to occur. The observed exchange rate depreciation and international inflation are co-symptoms of the shift in taste. An exception has been found so to the conventional wisdom of tracing two-way causality between external and internal depreciation of a currency.

Symmetrical proportionate change in taste by resident and non-resident was essential to the above conclusion. Non-symmetry taste changes can be satisfied only by an eventual currency-flow. The speculator accommodates in the short-run the shift in taste and determines a temporary exchange rate divergence from long-run trend.

If the desired total real reduction in guilder holdings was matched by a desired equal increase in say deutschmark exposure, non-symmetry is introduced, although second order in size. Dutch residents, having the heaviest exposure to guilders, are making the greatest reduction in absolute terms. If Dutch residents and non-residents want to switch 10 per cent of their guilder exposure into deutschmarks, the desired increase is necessarily of different proportion to present holdings of marks for German residents and non-residents. A source of international flow of capital is created.

CURRENCY COMPETITION AND CONTROLS

If shifts in currency taste have little effect on currency flows in or out of a state, it is surely desirable to exclude them from constraints in a programme to control net capital movements. A state may wish to limit net capital outflows for a variety of reasons yet it should not confuse that objective with currency protectionism. Capital flight is essentially different from currency flight. The former refers to a general desire by residents to shift wealth outside their political jurisdiction; the latter to a desired change in unit of account.

The Belgian dual exchange market permits currency competition whilst restricting net capital movements internationally. The franc market is divided into two tiers – financier and convertible: all current account type transactions are channelled through the convertible, all capital type both for residents and non-residents through the financier market. The financier franc is typically at a discount to the convertible, varying between 1 and 3 per cent, reflecting the constraining effect of the system of shifts of capital out of Belgium. Yet Belgians are permitted to hold and deal freely in foreign currencies provided financial transactions therein are conducted via the financier market.

Non-Belgians are not discouraged directly from holding or dealing in domestic francs other than by the wider bid-offer spreads which result. Capital controls normally maintain the real rate of return domestically, and thus the interest rate, at an uncompetitive level internationally. Capital is prevented from moving to earn higher returns abroad driving the marginal domestic rate up to the international level. Non-residents would normally find the currency of a country with capital controls unattractive. The dual exchange market has no such side-effects. The implicit tax on investment abroad by local residents is matched by an equal subsidy on inward investment by non-residents. So from their viewpoint the rate of interest on currency bought on the financial market is fully competitive with the US dollar and other freely tradable currencies.

By allocating trade and financial transactions to two separate markets the net outflow of capital is prevented. In a unified exchange market an overshooting depreciation generates a trade surplus equal to the desired capital outflow. But duality prevents transfer from trade account to capital account. Desired capital outflows drive the discount of the financial currency below the convertible and the convertible exchange rate and current account are in principle unaffected. A dual exchange market thus cuts off capital movements from their sources of fuel, current account imbalances. Desired capital flows are registered by the financial franc discount. No further reaction occurs.

NATURAL RESOURCE MONIES

Since the oil price explosion of 1973–4 there has grown an identifiable category of currencies supported by the high price of energy. The states of issue are favoured with large energy deposits. Their exchange rates share the common feature of having broken loose from the ties of purchasing power parity. Their interest rates do not reflect domestic inflation expectations. The currencies are small in size and their exchange markets are dominated by investment opinion which acknowledges that continuing appreciation relative to purchasing power parity level is necessary to generate a non-oil trade deficit to offset growing energy revenues. Yet pressure from the exchanges on the domestic credit market diminishes for longer maturities. Long-term interest rates continue to reflect mainly domestic inflation.

The most colourful examples are usually the most extreme. Here it is the Saudi riyal. The riyal has maintained its parity against the US dollar since 1975 despite an inflation rate 15 per cent greater in Saudi Arabia than in the US. Another example is the Dutch guilder which has remained strong against the West German mark despite a significantly higher inflation rate. Some may believe that sterling is becoming an energy currency with the advent of North Sea oil.

The differing pressure from exchange rate expectations at the short and long end of the credit market leads to a particularly sharp yield curve on energy monies. Borrowing energy money short and lending long is very attractive as illustrated in Table 1.5. The yield curve on non-energy currencies such as the dollar or deutschmark is very flat compared to on the riyal or guilder.

Conceptually short-term deposits in small energy monies may be thought of as traded goods. Competition is keen between them and

TABLE 1.5   Yield curves on energy monies compared Friday 8 July 1977

	1 wk	1 mo	3 mo	6 mo	1 yr	5 yr
Dutch guilder	$1\frac{1}{4}$	$2\frac{1}{4}$	$3\frac{1}{2}$	$4\frac{1}{2}$	$5\frac{3}{8}$	$7\frac{1}{2}$
Saudi riyal	$1\frac{1}{4}$	$1\frac{1}{2}$	$2\frac{1}{2}$	$3\frac{1}{2}$	$4\frac{1}{2}$	$8\frac{1}{2}$
Sterling	$7\frac{3}{4}$	$8\frac{3}{8}$	$9\frac{3}{8}$	$10\frac{5}{8}$	$10\frac{3}{4}$	$12\frac{1}{2}$
US dollar	$5\frac{3}{8}$	$5\frac{3}{4}$	$5\frac{3}{4}$	6	$6\frac{1}{4}$	7
W. German mark	$4\frac{1}{8}$	$4\frac{1}{16}$	$4\frac{1}{16}$	$4\frac{1}{8}$	$4\frac{5}{16}$	$5\frac{3}{4}$

Note: All rates are euro-, except for 5-year sterling which is domestic.

other denomination deposits and degree of substitutability fairly high. International money interest rate differentials tend therefore to reflect exchange rate expectations. Longer term deposits and bonds are more similar to non-traded goods, their market being less open to international influences as described. Borrowing short and lending long is like financing an inventory of non-traded goods with credit indexed to price of traded goods. As has been demonstrated a rising relative price of non-traded goods in terms of traded goods is a common feature of economies with growing output of high-priced energy. The profitability of the strategy of playing the yield curve in energy monies follows.

2 Dollar Market Satellites

The euro-deposit and currency markets form a solar system. Its sun is the US domestic money market. Planets include the euro-Swiss franc, US dollar and West German mark markets. Around each of these in turn satellites revolve. The euro-French franc market is a satellite of the forward dollar-franc currency market. All are under the common pull of the dollar sun which functions like Apollo's sun chariot. During its night of rest greater independence is possible for some planets and satellites. Order is restored when the clock strikes a certain hour and New York awakens. Such 'cinderella' markets are located in different time zones from the US. Independence is usually impossible for dollar markets which are exposed constantly to the sun's glare. Independent euro-dollar markets compete East-West across the earth not North-South. The division of business between financial centres from East to West occurs naturally. A longitudinal line was not drawn artificially like Pope Alexander VI's which divided the world between Spain and Portugal.

MARKET-MAKERS

The key to understanding the orbit of financial markets is the distinction between market-making and broking. The market-maker himself stands ready to buy or sell the currency or type of deposit in question. He charges for the service by fixing a margin between his bid and offer quotes. He risks capital as he holds an inventory – either positive or negative – of the instruments in which he is dealing. The broker by contrast intermediates simply between buyers and sellers or acts as agent for a market-maker.

When a bank dealer quotes $5\frac{1}{2}$–$5\frac{5}{8}$ per cent in the three month euro-dollar interbank market, he stands ready to pay $5\frac{1}{2}$ per cent on money deposited and lends, if requested, at $5\frac{5}{8}$ per cent. In technical language, $5\frac{1}{2}$ per cent and $5\frac{5}{8}$ per cent are the bank's bid and offer quotes respectively. Suppose towards the end of the day the bank has had more deposited with it than loans requested. An outlet for the excess deposits has to be found. It will shade down both its bid and offer quotes to say $5\frac{7}{16}-5\frac{9}{16}$ per cent so discouraging would-be depositors and encouraging borrowers. If near closing time the bank still has an excess of deposits, an outlet for them has to be found by approaching another market-maker. The bank's role is then that of a depositor, and it earns only $5\frac{1}{2}$ per cent, assuming that $5\frac{1}{2}-5\frac{5}{8}$ per cent is the second bank's bid-offer quote. The skill of successful market-making is to minimise the proportion of such off-loading transactions.

It can be seen that a market-making bank risks loss. It may have bid $5\frac{1}{2}$ per cent for deposits in the morning and find by midday that it has a net excess of deposits and the going bid-offer spread has dropped to $5\frac{1}{4}-5\frac{3}{8}$ per cent. A loss is so realized.

A broker in the euro-dollar market seeks the best quote from different market-makers on behalf of his client. The deal is then normally completed between the client and the market-maker. The broker charges a standard fee for his services.

Sometimes the broker enters the transactions as a principal. Having found an acceptable quote for his client he borrows the deposit in his own name. He re-lends it to the market-maker. The broker is thus a principal in two transactions. A bank may fulfil sometimes this second type of brokerage function – the provision of a credit guarantee for both the market-maker and his ultimate client. For example if a British bank was asked by a customer to quote for a euro-guilder deposit, it might approach a market-making Dutch bank. The guilder deposit accepted by the British bank would be re-lent to the Dutch market-maker.

PRIME, ASSOCIATE, SATELLITE AND CINDERELLA MARKETS

In a *prime market* are found competing market-makers. The euro-dollar deposit market in London is a prime market. Banks there maintain bid-offer spreads at which they are almost unreservedly prepared to do business. Extraordinarily large transactions or shaky credit may be refused. There are a sufficient number of market-makers and a sufficient amount of non-bank dollar loan and deposit business in London for it to be independent as a financial centre. The London dollar market's viability does not depend essentially on the existence of other centres with which to transact business, although a lot of such business is of course transacted. Independence is an essential quality of a prime market.

The dollar market in Amsterdam can usefully be contrasted with that in London. Euro-dollar business in the Netherlands is relatively thin. A bank which depended on Amsterdam-based business would find that its dealing inventory would turn over at a slower rate than for a London market-maker. The Amsterdam bank would have to quote a wider bid-offer spread to compensate for the overheads and risk on his extra inventory per unit turnover.

Who is going to deal with the above market-maker in Amsterdam when narrower dealing spreads are available in London? Only those transactors for whom the nuisance costs of dealing with London compared to Amsterdam are greater than the inferiority of the Dutch quote, say $\frac{1}{8}$ per cent. If the nuisance costs are less than $\frac{1}{8}$ per cent, business would all be done with London banks. The Amsterdam bank could not survive independently as a market-maker.

The Amsterdam dealer in dollars could try another line of business. He could set up as a broker and attract clients among those dealing directly with London market-makers. His brokerage charge must be less than the nuisance cost saved by his clients in dealing with Amsterdam rather than London. The form of nuisance cost is non-synchronisation of language and legal code in London and Amsterdam. A Dutch client prefers often dealing with another Dutchman in the same language and subject to a common law code than with a London bank. If most euro-dollar dealers in Amsterdam acted as brokers in the fashion described, the dollar market there would be termed a satellite of London.

Arbitrage between a prime and satellite market is not a meaningful concept. The broker in a satellite market is his own arbitrager. Suppose in the Amsterdam example brokerage costs were $\frac{1}{16}$ per cent, brokers would quote customers the best London spread $5\frac{1}{2}-\frac{5}{8}$ per cent plus their commission, making an 'all-in' quote of $5\frac{7}{16}-5\frac{11}{16}$ per cent.

The quotation of a bid-offer spread by a bank evidently does not imply that it is a market-maker. The bank may in reality be quoting another's bid-offer spread plus his brokerage charges. To discern whether a bank is a market-maker requires the lifting of the veil of the bid-offer spread and an investigation of whether a dealing inventory is being managed.

The would-be market-maker in Amsterdam had another choice. Finding that the depth of business in his city was insufficient to permit the generation of a competitive bid-offer spread he could have tried to get included in the London dealer network. He could attempt to establish relationships with London market-brokers and makers, so that as a matter of course he would be asked to quote often for business arising out of London. If he, together with others, were successful in being included in such a network, Amsterdam could be termed an *associate market* of London. The Amsterdam market would not have independent status. It could not exist without London.

The Amsterdam market would however support a group of market-makers distinguishing it from a satellite. Brokers in London and the Netherlands would approach Amsterdam market-makers for quotes. Arbitrage between the Amsterdam and London dollar markets would not be meaningful. They would be minor and major parts of an integrated dollar market.

The phenomenon of *cinderella markets* is due to the earth being round. The euro-Canadian dollar market in London is cinderella. In the morning market-making occurs in London where the difference in time-zone prevents the competition of narrower bid-offer quotes in the broader Canadian market. By afternoon, when Canada is operating, market-makers in London find it impossible to match quotes in Canada other than by acting as broker for the Canadian market.

SYSTEM ILLUSTRATED

Tables 2.1, 2.2 and 2.3 illustrate systems of prime, associate satellite and cinderella markets in foreign exchange, money, credit, commodities and equities. Some of the entries will be looked at in more detail in this book. Some are illustrated now in order to develop further the concept of market systems.

DOLLAR-POUND FOREIGN EXCHANGE MARKET

The prime markets for trading dollars against pounds are in London

TABLE 2.1   Markets in foreign exchange

Title	Prime Market	Associate Market	Satellite Market	Cinderella Market
$-DM	Frankfurt London New York	Munich		
$-£	London New York		Amsterdam	
forward $-Saudi riyal	Bahrain	Jeddah London		
$-C$	Toronto New York Montreal			London
Cross currency market	$-DM, $-£		DM-£	
Banknote market Basel	Sw. fr.-$, £-Sw. fr.		£-$ banknote market Basel	

and New York. What happens if a trader approaches his bank in Amsterdam and asks it to quote a rate of exchange for dollars into sterling? It may make a bid-offer quote, but its role will certainly not be that of a market-maker. The amount of two-way business between dollars and sterling direct is much too thin in Amsterdam for a bank there which ran an inventory in dollars against pounds to be able to quote a bid-offer spread that would be competitive with London. Rather, the Amsterdam bank will seek a dollar-pound quote from a market-maker in London and add on his brokerage charges. The dollar-pound market in Amsterdam is a satellite of the London foreign exchange market.

FORWARD DOLLAR-SAUDI RIYAL MARKET

The forward dollar-riyal market is unusual in that the money market situated in the country of currency issue, Saudi Arabia, is an associate of one outside in Bahrain. Financial activities are much

TABLE 2.2   Markets in money and credit

Title	Prime Market	Associate Market	Satellite Market	Cinderella Market
Domestic US money market	New York	Chicago		
$ interbank term deposits	Euro-$s	Term Fed. funds		
Euro-$	London, Paris	Zurich, Luxembourg		Asian $s
Euro-DMs	Luxembourg	London		
Swiss francs	Euro-Swiss francs		Domestic interbank Swiss francs	
Guilders	Euro-guilders	Dutch money markets		
Belgian franc convertible	Euro-$, $-franc convertible		Euro-franc convertible	
Belgian franc financier	domestic Belgian money market		Euro-franc financier	
Saudi Riyal	Bahrain		Jeddah	

better developed in Bahrain than in Saudi: Bahrain is a fast-growing offshore centre and many foreign banks have set up there using sophisticated dealing practices. Most of the foreign exchange business done in Saudi Arabia is on a broker basis through Bahrain. One Saudi bank is a market-maker with associate market status to Bahrain.

DOLLAR-CANADIAN DOLLAR EXCHANGE MARKET

The Prime markets are Toronto, New York and Montreal. London is a cinderella market. In the morning (London time) the North Atlantic markets are closed. A market-maker in London will attract business even though natural

TABLE 2.3 Markets in commodities and equities

Title	Prime Market	Associate Market	Satellite Market	Cinderella Market
Platinum	New York			London
Copper	London New York			
Silver	New York London Zurich			
$-LME copper	**£-LME** copper, $- £		**$-LME** copper	
US equities	New York			London Zurich
Copper borrowing	Spot LME copper, forward LME copper		Borrowing outside 'rings'	Borrowing inside 'rings'

thinness necessitates him forming a wider bid-ask spread than his North Atlantic counterparts could. Many transactors located in Europe prefer to complete business in the morning and will pay the wider spreads necessary.

GUILDER MONEY MARKET

Interbank business in guilder deposits in the Netherlands is thin. The euro-guilder market, located mainly in London and Luxembourg, is broader. The Dutch domestic interbank market is an associate of the euro-guilder market. Brokers in the latter will often seek quotes from Amsterdam and Rotterdam banks and *vice versa*. Dutch central bank regulations have at times restricted the free flow of funds from the euro-guilder market, but by 1977 they were of minor importance.

US EQUITIES

The prime marketplace is Wall Street. Many European investors wish to deal before New York opens. Independent markets exist to cater for their needs in London and Zurich as well as lesser centres. When trading on Wall Street starts European market-makers are metamorphosed into brokers. They tend then to transmit orders directly through New York Stock Exchange members rather than dealing in their own inventory.

INTERBANK BUSINESS

The problems of measuring the euro-markets are manifold. Not the least is that of separating genuine commercial business from dealings between market-makers themselves. In the smaller and younger financial centres, such as Singapore, a high proportion of business is interbank and is largely with banks in other centres. Problems of definition and measurement can be illuminated by appeal to the prime-satellite market concept. Three propositions are developed.

1. *As the number of banks in a financial centre increase, for a given amount of non-bank business, interbank business between local banks increases*

The first proposition follows from statistical considerations. Most banks are market-makers. As the number of market-makers competing for the same amount of business increases they will tend to deal more with each other. The amount of non-bank business per market-maker decreases and so does the variability of the ratio of excess inventory (positive or negative) to non-bank turnover. Thinner business reduces the chance of offsetting funds deposited with borrowers who approach him, and conversely. More often towards the end of the business day, market-makers will find themselves off-loading excess inventory on to other market-makers. The transactions are effected in the interbank market. In that market one bank (the approached) acts as market-maker, the other as his client.

The excess positive inventory which one market-maker finds himself with towards the end of the day will tend to have its counterpart negative inventory with another market-maker. Both of these enter the interbank market as clients and will be 'matched' most likely indirectly by a third-party market-maker. The amount of business for market-makers does not therefore shrink proportionately to the increase in this number. Market-making for market makers is a secondary source of turnover that increases with the number of market-makers.

A symptom of growing maturity of a financial centre is a declining proportion of interbank business. A high proportion must imply a basic non-competitiveness except for special factors. Each non-bank transaction must be supported by a higher proportion of interbank transactions. The cost of manufacturing deposits and loans for non-bank clients is therefore greater.

2. *As non-bank business increases in a financial centre with a constant number of banks, the proportion of interbank business within the centre and with banks in other centres decreases*

Very young financial centres do not enjoy the depth of business necessary for independent market-makers to operate profitably. The first banks arriving there will act as brokers, often for their own offices in mature centres. The sponsors of new offshore markets are keen to attract branches of large international banks. Their low cost brokerage helps to attract business in the first stage of a centre's development. International banking connections are vital if progress is to be made to the second stage where associate status to a larger market is gained. The final stage is marked by the blossoming into a prime market.

The Bahrain Monetary Authority, one of the most recent sponsors of a new centre has been very selective in granting operating licences. Banks with ready access to market-makers in major financial centres have been favoured. Most business in Bahrain is still of a broking nature. A bank asked to quote for a dollar deposit would base it on that of his correspondent in another centre adding some brokerage charge. The deposit would be booked as a liability of the branch which would have an offsetting interbank asset with its correspondent outside.

A large proportion of business taking the form of interbank transactions with other financial centres is a feature of a satellite or associate market. In the latter well-connected banks act as associates of another centre. Brokers with whom they have established relationships there seek quotes on both loans and deposits. If such business is sufficiently deep, it can support a competitive bid-offer spread by bank market-makers in the new centre.

3. *Increasing the number of banks in a financial centre, for a given volume of*

business, tends to increase the proportion of interbank business with other financial centres

The proposition is a simple corollary of the previous one. More banks imply less non-bank potential business for each, necessitating wider bid-offer spreads to justify the market-making function. The maturing of the financial centre, symptomised by banks shedding their caterpillar broker form for that of the market-making butterfly, is delayed. Promoters of new offshore centres should ration strictly new banking permits if they want to hasten the take-off point into prime status for a given prospective growth rate of total business.

TABLE 2.4   Asian dollar market: assets and liabilities of ACUS
1968–72 US $m

		Assets				Liabilities		
			Interbank funds				Interbank funds	
End year	Loans to non banks	Total	in Singa-pore	outside Singa-pore	Deposits of non-banks	Total	in Singa-pore	outside Singa-pore
1968	1·4	29·0	n.a.	n.a.	17·8	12·6	n.a.	n.a.
1969	0·9	120·5	n.a.	n.a.	97·9	23·7	n.a.	n.a.
1970	13·9	370·2	13·1	357·1	243·7	141·0	5·7	135·3
1971	188·8	850·8	38·5	812·3	237·9	811·2	56·4	754·8
1972	600·9	2331·8	99·4	2231·7	398·7	2551·0	145·0	2405·1

Source: Singapore Monetary Authority.

An examination of statistics on the growth of the Asian dollar market in Singapore illustrates the three propositions. Table 2.4 shows that both the proportion of interbank loan business within and outside Singapore decreased during the formative years of its creation as a financial centre, 1968–72. Analysis of Singapore's deposit business is complicated by the one-way nature of dollar business in the early years. Singapore was essentially a broker placing non-bank dollar deposits in other financial centres. Two-way business can be dated from 1971. The number of banks has also expanded rapidly since then so the proportion of interbank deposit business has increased rather than declined.

ONE-WAY FINANCIAL CENTRES

The kindest environment for market-making is good two-way
business, between deposits and loans. If asymmetry exists, such as
many more non-bank borrowers than depositors, then the successful
market-maker will have to build a network of business contacts in
other centres who will often ask him to quote on deposit business.
Otherwise the market-maker would tend to find that he had
repeatedly large excess negative deposit inventories and was having
to off-load position with market-makers in other centres at the
'wrong' side of their bid-offer spread. He would have to quote a
wider bid-ask spread to cover this probability than more favoured
counterparts elsewhere. Brokerage rather than market-making
tends to prevail in one-way centres and the take-off into a prime
from a satellite market is delayed.

In theory though it should be possible for banks in a one-way
centre to attract interbank market-making business in the opposite
direction to prevailing non-bank business in the aggregate of other
centres. In the total euro-market, combining all financial centres,
non-bank business must be equal in both directions. If a centre tends
to suffer from one-way non-bank trading, another is likely to
complain of business being predominantly in the opposite direction.
Market-makers in the two centres would gain from building up
networks of associates in each other's market. The two would thus
become associate markets of each other. Together they would form
a prime market rather than being satellites of an entirely separate
prime market.

A variety of factors can cause business to have a one-way
tendency. A centre may have stringent laws concerning bank
secrecy which encourages the placing of deposits yet have no
natural loan demand. Conversely exchange restrictions may prevent local residents from placing dollar deposits while they may be
encouraged to borrow dollars.

Zurich is an example of a centre of the first type, London and
Paris of the second. Yet London has countered successfully its
deposit side weakness. By developing the only market in negotiable
dollar certificates of deposit outside the US, and exempting interest
on dollar deposits from all tax, London has attracted much non-
resident dollar deposit business. Tokyo by contrast has had no such
success. The Japanese authorities have until recently restricted
severely the holding of dollar deposits by their residents. Yet almost

all of Japan's trade is financed in dollars and Tokyo banks have a large catchment of local clients for dollar loans. The Japanese authorities have made difficult a remedy for Tokyo's natural bias. Dollar deposits were not exempted from withholding tax and the growth of offshore money market activities has been discouraged officially.

Luxembourg as a financial centre is an *entrepôt* between other one-way business centres, itself enjoying two-way trade. Swiss banks place funds in the interbank market there: Paris and London banks borrow there to meet their natural excess loan demand. German banks use Luxembourg as a source of Euro-DM finance. The high proportion of interbank business in Luxembourg reflects its *entrepôt* character in the euro-interbank markets rather than being a symptom of satellite existence. The exception demonstrates again the intense difficulties of statistical investigation of euro-market structure.

FOREIGN EXCHANGE

With the eventual demise of the Bretton Woods international monetary system in 1971 the special legal pre-eminence of the US dollar came to an end. Yet today the dollar remains the key pivot through which most foreign exchange business is done.

If a bank in Zurich for example is asked to quote a rate of exchange for guilders against Swiss francs, it will base its calculation on a combined Swiss franc-dollar, dollar-guilder quote. The bank will probably itself be a market-maker in Swiss francs against dollars. As a broker it will seek a dollar-guilder quote from a market-maker in the Dutch foreign exchange market, most probably a Dutch bank. It will combine the two quotes into a single Swiss franc-guilder spread, adding brokerage charges. The Swiss franc-guilder market is a satellite of the dollar-Swiss franc and dollar-guilder prime markets.

Some older textbooks on foreign exchange discuss at some length the possibilities of triangular arbitrage; it exists now rarely in practice. An essential property of satellites is their non-independence. Arbitrage between the satellite and its prime market is not meaningful. Quotes in the satellite are themselves formed by arbitrage (brokerage) with the prime market. Independent arbitrage does not occur between the Swiss franc-guilder market, and the guilder-dollar, dollar-Swiss franc markets. The customer of the Swiss bank, in asking for a guilder-Swiss franc quote, should acknowledge that he is using the bank partly as a broker. The alternative would be for him to seek two quotes from different market-makers, one for guilder-dollar, the other for dollar-Swiss francs and combine the two himself.

Market-makers are not to be found in a guilder-Swiss franc exchange market because it is thin. The bid-offer spread that a market-maker would have to quote given the low ratio of turnover to his average inventory (hence risk) would be wider than the combination of spreads on guilder-dollars, dollar-Swiss franc deals.

The broadest exchange market, hence keenest quotes, for a currency against the dollar is found typically in the country of issue. Banks' commercial clients there generate potentially the largest turnover relative to inventories. The keenest dollar-deutschmark quote is often to be gained from a bank market-maker in Germany.

Three major exceptions at least exist to the identification of the broadest exchange market with the country issuing the currency. They are London, Zurich and New York. London and Zurich have developed reputations as international currency market centres. There is sufficient non-resident participation for these cities to make competitive markets in US dollars against major currencies. In contrast sufficient depth of business does not exist in Frankfurt for a bank to make a market competitively there for dollars against third currencies. A Frankfurt quote for dollars against pounds would be made in capacity of broker for London or Zurich.

New York's place in the world's currency markets is unique. As all currencies are traded against the US dollar, and the US accounts for the largest proportion of world trade, market-makers in New York are found for all currencies against the dollar. Compared to Zurich or London the variety of markets depends not on the development over decades of non-resident participation, but rather on significant natural local commercial interest in all currencies.

In recent years Hong Kong has grown into an international currency market. Market-makers exist in the major European currencies against the US dollar. Hong Kong's development has been fast, fostered by the protection of a large time zone difference from other world markets.

Innovations in market-making can be as remarkable as in the world of technology, but less widely perceived. It is very often hard to discover the reason for the timing of their introduction. For several years now the relationship of the West German mark to the Swiss franc has been more stable than that of the Swiss franc to the US dollar. Germany is Switzerland's largest trading partner and a substantial potential two-way trade of francs against marks exists. Although such a market would be thinner than dollars against francs, and the ratio of turnover to inventory smaller, the risk of exchange loss to the market-maker would be lower. He might therefore be able to support a lower bid-offer spread than the combined dollar-franc, dollar-deutschmark spreads plus brokerage. Entrepreneural courage would be required to set up as the first market-maker in francs against deutschmarks and to quote a lower spread than the two dollar markets combined. Losses would be made at first until sufficient clients were attracted. Market-making in currency exchanges not involving the US dollar is an innovation to which to look forward. Independent cross exchange markets have existed historically. In the interwar period banks made markets in both pounds and dollars against many other currencies.

MARKET-MAKING IN BANKNOTES

Features of foreign exchange markets in banknotes differ in some major respects from those in bank deposits (drafts). The role of the US dollar is not pivotal. Indeed exchange markets for greenbacks are often satellites of two prime markets. The essential difference of banknote market organisation stems from the comparative high costs of transporting banknotes between different centres.

In Switzerland – one of the most important banknote markets – prime markets exist in most notes traded against the Swiss franc. The bid-offer spread on 'related' currencies is narrower than against the US dollar: the spread on Swiss francs-West German mark is less than on Swiss franc-dollars. Germany is Switzerland's largest neighbour and there is a lot of tourist and commercial traffic between the two countries. The comparative size of spreads is indicative not only of differing market breadth, but also of costs of delay in banking excess inventories (see Chapter 1, p. 8). No-one in Switzerland will make a market in dollar banknotes against French francs for example. The volume of business would be much too small and the spread greater than on the combination of Swiss franc-French franc, Swiss franc-US dollar quotes. The rate of exchange will be inferior to French franc-dollar quotes in France.

The impossibility of independent banknote market-making between two currencies not including one issued by the state where the market is located is in sharp contrast to market-making in bank drafts. The difference is due to relative transport costs of bank drafts and banknotes.

An interesting banknote market is that for French francs against Spanish peseta in Andorra. Andorra has no legal tender; francs and peseta circulate side by side and are used about equally. The spread in the exchange market of one against the other is reportedly substantially lower than in either Madrid or Paris. Yet spreads on either currency against the US dollar are much wider in Andorra than in either metropolis.

EXOTIC EURO-CURRENCIES

Most of us realise that, if we want fresh strawberries in December, we must pay a premium over their price when produced under natural conditions in the summer. It is less widely understood that a premium is paid for being able to borrow or lend minor euro-currencies compared to dealing in the three dream monies – Swiss francs, dollars and deutschmarks.

Business in minor euro-currencies, such as British pounds and French francs, is thin. Often markets in these euro-currencies have the characteristics of satellites of the foreign exchange and euro-dollar market. A bank in Paris, asked to quote for euro-pounds at a time when trading in the euro-pounds is thin, might find itself able to formulate a narrower bid-offer spread by acting as a broker between the foreign exchange and euro-dollar market than as a market-maker in euro-pounds. As a broker he would manufacture his euro-pound bid rate by calculating his total return from selling the pounds placed with him for dollars, investing the dollars in a euro-dollar deposit and buying pounds forward for dollars to protect his exposure. He would assume that he was transacting on the adverse side of all bid-offer spreads and subtract his brokerage charge. He would manufacture his euro-pound offer rate by calculating the cost of borrowing dollars, selling dollars spot for pounds (to deliver to client) and buying pound forward for dollars to protect his position. Again he would assume that he was transacting on the adverse side of all bid-offer spreads and *add* his brokerage charge. Dealing costs on executing simultaneously a spot and forward exchange transaction with the same market-maker are lower than on effecting two separate deals: making a market in spot-and-forward combinations is low risk.

The narrowness of the euro-pound and franc markets is attributable to exchange restrictions that prevent the free flow of funds to and from the much larger domestic credit markets. Associate status for those euro-markets with their respective domestic markets is not therefore possible.

The interest rate parity theorem is one of the oldest in currency economics. It states that interest rates on different currencies differ by the forward discount of one against the other provided no exchange restrictions exist. In the context of the euro-markets the theorem would predict for example that euro-French franc three-month interest rates equal three-month euro-dollar interest rates plus the three-month forward discount of the franc against the dollar. If that relationship did not hold, it is argued conventionally that arbitrage profit could be made from borrowing francs, selling them spot for dollars, investing in dollar deposits and buying francs three-month forward for dollars or *vice versa*.

In the context of minor euro-currencies the interest rate parity theorem states an identity rather than a predicted equilibrium relation. As discussed above euro-franc transactions are likely to be satellite to the dollar-franc spot market, dollar-franc forward market and the euro-dollar market. Euro-franc rates are themselves quoted on the basis of arbitrage (broking) between these three markets. No independent arbitrage is therefore possible between the euro-franc and the other three markets.

The satellite nature of minor euro-currency markets confounds further difficulties of measuring them. Euro-pound, euro-franc and other similar business can be dug out from below the accounting edifice of euro-dollar loans and deposits. Consider a bank which, having been requested to lend euro-pounds by a client, borrows dollars, sells them spot for pounds and sells the pound forward for dollars for delivery at the maturity date of the loan. An accounting statement of the bank's position would show on its asset side a euro-pound loan, matched on its liability side by a euro-dollar deposit. The Bank for International Settlements and other agencies that measure the euro-markets would inevitably include the euro-pound loan in the asset total of the euro-pound market and the euro-dollar deposit in the liability total of the euro-dollar market.

The accounting definition of each euro-market does not distinguish genuine deposit and loan business. When a bank borrows euro-dollars and sells pounds forward for dollars to make a euro-pound loan, it is in effect borrowing euro-pounds. The bank obtains that euro-pound finance by the satellite market operation already described. A similar distinction can be made in analysing the bank's asset composition. If spot and forward positions were considered together, to discover satellite euro-currency loans some euro-dollar loans would be categorised as minor euro-currency loans. The revised measures of euro-market size for each currency shall be termed here 'swap-inclusive'.

A 'swap' is a technical term in the language of the foreign exchange markets. When a bank sells dollars spot for pounds and buys simultaneously dollars forward for pounds, the combined spot-and-forward operation is called a dollar for pound 'swap'.

The swap-inclusive measure of a euro-currency compared to the accounting measure is demonstrated in Figure 2.1. The proportion

Assets		Liabilities	
'Swapped out' euro-£	X	'Swapped in' Euro-£	A
Euro-£ loans	Y	Euro-£ deposits	B
	X + Y		A + B

FIG. 2.1   Swap inclusive measure of minor euro-currency market

of swap business to total is analogous to the proportion of interbank business with other financial centres in an examination of the primeness of a given centre. The reader will remember that a high proportion of intercentre business often indicated that the centre in question was a satellite of another. Similarly, when considering the relation between different denominated euro-currency markets, a high proportion of swap business in a currency suggests that its deposit market is a satellite of larger euro-currency markets. For example euro-French franc business is almost entirely 'swap'. This indicates that the euro-franc market is a satellite of the euro-dollar, forward dollar-franc and spot dollar-franc markets.

Euro-markets in the three 'dream' currencies – Swiss francs, West German marks and US dollars – are prime. The amount of swap business is small and is due to arbitrage rather than market-making operations. A bank asked to quote for euro-dollars would be uncompetitive with a straight market-maker in euro-dollars if it formed a spread by acting as broker with the spot-deutschmark, forward dollar-deutschmark and euro-deutschmark deposit market. Expressed more familiarly, it would be rare for a bank to fund a euro-dollar loan by swapping in deutschmarks. Further it is not standard practice for swaps to be used to meet demand for deutschmark and Swiss franc loans or to create deutschmark and Swiss franc deposits. All three euro-currency markets are sufficiently broad to support market-making independently of the foreign exchange markets. Covered interest arbitrage between the euro-deutschmark, euro-Swiss franc and euro-US dollar markets can and does occur. In practice arbitrage is profitable only for banks that are market-makers both in deposits and the respective foreign exchange markets.

The creation of minor euro-currencies can be demonstrated to involve the manufacture of dollar assets or liabilities by using a swap operation. It would never be economical for a bank to satisfy genuine dollar deposit or loan demand by swapping funds from other euro-currency markets. The necessity of doing that to manufacture minor euro-currencies explains why they are termed here as exotic. An extra cost is imposed on transactors wishing minor rather than dream currency denomination.

The unnatural process of minor euro-currency creation deserves more attention. Insight can be gained from re-grouping the set of transactions that combine to make, say, a euro-pound loan. The bank requested to lend euro-pounds to a client, borrows dollars, sells them spot for pounds and lends these. It protects its foreign exchange exposure by selling pounds forward for dollars. The transactions can be segregated into two sets: (1) borrowing euro-dollars (2) selling dollars spot for pounds, lending the pounds at the euro-pound interest rate and buying dollars forward for pounds.

The bank is thus demonstrated to have matched the euro-dollar deposit with an unnatural dollar asset which has been formed by *selling dollars spot for pounds, lending pounds and buying dollars forward*. The bank could not quote competitively for euro-dollar deposit business if it intended to act simply as broker in the dollar-pound exchange markets and euro-pound market to create a satellite euro-dollar. Such a brokerage creation of euro-dollars has been revealed when euro-pound loans are matched by euro-dollar deposits. The cost of the unnatural creation of the euro-dollar asset underlying the bank's euro-pound loan is borne by the client who wants pound rather than dollar denomination of his loan. The cost equals the difference in yield between authentic euro-dollar assets and the yield obtainable by swapping them out into euro-pounds – by selling the dollars spot for pounds, investing in euro-pounds and buying dollars forward.

Dividing lines drawn in market analysis are often expositary rather than absolute. Euro-currency markets can be ranged in a continuum from minor to major. At one end are found clustered the US dollar, West German mark and Swiss franc. Progressing towards the minor end is encountered the French franc, sterling, then Belgian (convertible) francs and yen.

In euro-sterling and euro-francs some independent market-making is sometimes to be found. When business is active banks will quote spreads not based on the intention of offsetting with swaps. Their spreads will then be narrower than when calculated on the satellite transactions. In the euro-yen and euro-convertible Belgian franc markets, no independent market-making exists. They are at the far end of the major-minor euro-currency continuum.

BID-OFFER SPREADS ON EURO-CURRENCIES

The bid-offer spread in a euro-currency market is not independent of the spread between that currency's swap points. The swap points on euro-deutschmarks for example are those that would be formed as a satellite operation of the spot and forward dollar-deutschmark markets and the euro-dollar markets. More precisely the 'bid' deutschmark deposit swap point is the return from selling marks spot for dollars, investing in a euro-dollar deposit (at bid rate) and selling dollars forward for deutschmarks. The 'offer' deutschmark swap point is the cost of borrowing dollars (at offer rate), selling dollars spot for deutschmarks and buying dollars forward for deutschmarks.

On major euro-currencies the spread between bid and offer rates is firmly less than between the dollar swap points. Someone who formed quotes on a satellite basis would, in general, be non-competitive, as is illustrated for euro-deutschmarks in Figure 2.2. An analogy in the dimension of space rather than currency would be the non-competitiveness of someone quoting euro-dollar rates in London as a broker of the Asian-dollar market in Singapore. Similarly a bank quoting euro-dollar rates by broking between the euro-deutschmark, spot and forward dollar-deutschmark exchange markets would normally be non-competitive.

In exceptional circumstances, a bank will intend to arbitrage

25 July 1977, opening quotes
   3-month euro-$s   5·75   −5·87%
      DM/$ spot   2·2550−2·2560
      DM/$ 3 months   115−110 swap

Swap points

Bid: $\left[\dfrac{1}{2 \cdot 2550} \times 1 \cdot 014375 \times 2 \cdot 2435 - 1 \right]$ 400 = 3·64

Offer: $\left[\dfrac{1}{2 \cdot 2560} \times 1 \cdot 014688 \times 2 \cdot 2450 - 1 \right]$ 400 = 3·89

A satellite euro-DM quote would thus be 3·64–3·89%.
In reality the 3-month euro-DM quote opened at 3·71–3·84%, well within the swap points.

FIG. 2.2   Euro-DM rates within swap points

when quoting for euro-deutschmark or euro-Swiss franc business. That occurs when one side of the bid-offer spread on deposits is outside a swap point. The bank would then intend to offset a deposit with a swap in the opposite direction thereby exploiting the arbitrage profit opportunity. Because spreads are narrowest in euro-dollars foreign exchange arbitrage profit is never present for dollar deposit market-makers. If either side of the dollar bid-offer quote slipped outside say its dollar-deutschmark 'swap point', a significant arbitrage profit must already exist from quoting for euro-deutschmarks with the intention of offsetting with a dollar-mark swap. Significant arbitrage profit opportunities would be extraordinary in the highly competitive major foreign exchange and euro-markets.

The swap points determine a minimum spread for euro-currency rates, even in the three major denominations – Swiss francs, West German and US dollars. It must not be cheaper to borrow deutschmarks at the offer rate, sell them spot for dollars and invest in euro-dollars at the bid rate, than to sell deutschmarks forward for dollars. The two resulting exposures to exchange and interest risk are identical and arbitrage by banks will ensure that the inequality holds. Similarly it must not be cheaper to borrow dollars at the offer rate, sell them spot for deutschmarks and invest in euro-deutschmarks at the bid rate, than to buy deutschmarks forward for dollars. Together these two inequalities determine minimum spread for euro-deutschmark rates. In practice the euro-deutschmark bid-offer spread is somewhere between this minimum and the maximum possible fixed by the dollar-deutschmark swap points.

During a crisis in the foreign exchange markets, bid-offer spreads in the spot-and-forward currency markets widen because the risk of inventory holding to market-makers increases. The wider spread in the currency markets widens the minimum spread in the corresponding euro-market. A spillover effect of hectic conditions on the deutschmark-dollar axis is wider dealing spread on euro-deutschmark transactions.

EURO-BELGIAN FRANC MARKET

The euro-Belgian franc market provides an interesting further insight of the possible relationship of satellite to prime markets. As already described in Chapter 1 (p. 29) the Belgian franc currency market is divided into two tiers – the financier and convertible. Corresponding to the division in the currency market is a duality in the euro-deposit market. In London euro-convertible and euro-financier franc deposits and loans are made. Both markets are satellites but of different prime markets.

The euro-financier franc market is a satellite of the domestic Belgian money market. Flows between the two are completely unrestricted and involve no foreign exchange transaction. When a Belgian transfers francs to a financier account in London the bank there has at first a financier-franc claim on a Belgian bank. The market in financier francs is too thin to justify independent market-making. Instead a bank on receiving a euro-financier franc deposit will act simply as a money broker to the Belgian market, on-lending it there and quoting the bid rate in Brussels minus a brokerage charge. A similar procedure is followed to manufacture euro-financier franc loans.

The bank could alternatively have formed a euro-financier franc quote by broking between the euro-dollar market and the spot and forward dollar-financier franc markets. The bid offer spread would equal the difference between the two 'swap points' from those markets. In practice the spreads so formed would normally be uncompetitive with those arrived at by broking with the domestic Belgium money market. The bank dealing in euro-financier franc deposits has a choice of one of two sets of prime markets around which to orbit and must select the least costly.

The euro-convertible franc market is a satellite of the convertible franc-dollar spot and forward exchange markets and the euro-dollar market. Direct flows between the euro-convertible franc market and the domestic Belgian money market are not possible. A Belgian must first sell his francs for dollars in the financier exchange market, then sell those dollars for francs in the convertible market. Sometimes he will receive as little as 96 convertible francs for 100 financier (domestic) francs.The London bank forms a keener quote as a broker than he could as an independent market-maker in convertible francs.

MARKET FAILURE

The positive scientist confines his examination to the world as it exists. Imagining the world as it could be is a luxury that is denied him. No such self-denying ordinance is proposed here. Having examined a number of forward and euro-markets and their interrelationship it is tempting to consider why so few exist. Why is there no euro-market in Australian dollars? Why do most forward exchange markets extend only up to one year? The concept of prime and market satellites is again helpful in answering these questions.

NON-EXISTENCE OF FORWARD EXCHANGE MARKETS

Most forward exchange markets do not exist for maturities of more than one year ahead. Where they exist they are very narrow. For short maturities importers and exporters use forward markets. Their depth can support independent market-making.

The exchange risk protection that a trader gains by selling or buying a currency forward, can also be gained by composite borrowing and lending transactions. Suppose a German importer wishes to hedge payment of a dollar invoice in three months' time. He could either buy dollars forward for deutschmarks for delivery in three months, or he could borrow deutschmarks, sell them spot and invest in a three-month euro-dollar deposit. On its maturing he would apply the proceeds to invoice payment. Covered interest arbitrage ensures that the costs of both operations are similar, but not identical. If the three-month forward premium on deutschmarks (against dollars) was significantly greater than the euro-deutschmark, euro-dollar three-month differential interest rate, pure arbitrage profit could be made from borrowing three-month deutschmarks, selling them spot for dollars, investing in three-month dollars and buying deutschmarks three months forward. The relationship so described between interest rates and the forward exchange marks is the subject of the interest rate parity theorem. Unfortunately simple statements of it ignore often the important question of transaction costs. If these are considered, the theorem states a tendency rather than an equality.

Forward exchange rate spreads will usually be less than those between the costs of the corresponding composite transactions. In the deutschmark-dollar example, the bid-offer spread on three-month forward dollars against deutschmarks will be less than between (1) borrowing three-month deutschmarks, selling them spot for dollars, investing in three-month dollars and (2) borrowing three-month dollars, selling them spot for deutschmarks, investing in three-month deutschmarks. (Bid-offer spreads are compared as a percentage of the dollar value of invoice being hedged.) Independent market-makers in three-month forward dollar-deutschmarks can out-compete someone who formed forward quotes as a satellite of the euro-deutschmark, euro-dollar and spot dollar-deutschmarks markets.

As maturities lengthen, forward markets narrow, and they tend to become satellites of the euro-markets and spot exchange market. Beyond one year, business is too narrow for an independent market-maker to compete. A bank which quotes a two-year deutschmark-dollar rate intends to offset its position immediately rather than run an inventory in forward dollar-deutschmarks and wait to find a client wanting to transact in the opposite direction. If requested to quote a rate for a customer buying dollars two years forward for deutschmark, it will calculate the cost of itself borrowing two-year deutschmarks selling spot for dollars and lending two-year dollars. The deutschmark loan principle plus two years interest thereon plus brokerage charge will be its deutschmark quote for selling dollars two years forward equal in amount to the dollar investment plus two years' interest. So the two-year forward deutschmark-dollar market is a satellite of the two-year deutschmark and dollar money markets and spot dollar-deutschmark market.

FORWARD MARKETS IN RESTRICTED CURRENCIES

Independent market-making persists sometimes for longer maturities in currencies of restricted tradability. Independent market-makers are found in the forward dollar-pound market for up to four-year maturities. The broking transactions that would be necessary for the forward dollar-pound market to be a satellite are impeded by restrictions on sterling's convertibility. A dealer in forward sterling is limited in his borrowing of domestic sterling to sell spot for foreign currencies. A potentially cheaper way of manufacturing two- three- and four-year forward sterling is barred thus and more expensive independent market-making is effectively protected.

No restrictions apply to the borrowing of euro-pounds. In theory, two- three- and four-year forward sterling could be a satellite market of the two-year euro-pound, two-year euro-dollar and spot dollar-pound market. A bank asked to quote for two-year forward sterling would intend to offset its position by borrowing two-year euro-pound, selling spot for dollars and investing in two-year euro-dollars or conversely. In practice independent market-making in two to four-year euro-pounds would be much more expensive than in two to four-year forward pounds. Hence the two to four-year forward pound is an independent market whilst the two to four-year euro-pound is a satellite market of the two to four-year forward pound, spot dollar-pound and two to four-year euro-dollar markets. The satellite relationship between those markets is identical to the one already described for 0–12 months euro-pounds.

The euro-dollar market is unique in having prime markets for one to four-year maturities. For all other euro-currencies markets in maturities of greater than one year assume a satellite nature (see Table 2.5). The satellite relationships are different for currencies with restricted tradability from those with free tradability. The British pound and deutschmark are taken as examples of each type.

Business in two to four-year euro-deutschmarks is very narrow. Until 1978, non-resident placements in the Frankfurt 2–4 year money market were not penalised. Independent market-makers could not compete in two to four-year euro-deutschmarks with banks that re-lent or borrowed in Frankfurt funds deposited (or lent) in Luxembourg (the centre of the euro-deutschmark market).

Business in two to four-year euro-pounds is also very narrow. But banks operating in euro-pounds have limited access only to borrowing in the much broader domestic pound market. Therefore they cannot attach themselves to it as satellites as do banks operating in two to four-year euro-deutschmarks. Instead they

TABLE 2.5   Prime and satellite forward markets

Market	Maturity	
	0–12 months	*2–4 years*
Forward DM-$	Prime	Satellite of 1. spot $-DMs 2. 2–4 yr euro-$s 3. 2–4 yr domestic DM money markets
Euro-DMs	Prime	Satellite of 2–4 yr. domestic DM money market
Forward £-$	Prime	Prime
Euro- £s	Satellite of 1. spot $ - £s 2. 0–1 yr euro-$s 3. 0–1 yr forward $ - £	Satellite of 1. spot $ - £s 2. 2–4 yr euro-$s 3. 2–4 yr forward $ - £

become satellites of the forward dollar-pound, spot dollar pound and euro-deposit market.

NON-EXISTENCE OF EURO-MARKETS

Besides the euro-currencies so far discussed euro-markets can also be found in Hong Kong dollars, yen and Italian lire. They are 100 per cent satellite markets. Why could the 'swap' technique not be used to generate euro-forms for other currencies?

Could an enterprising bank in Singapore not initiate a euro-Australian dollar market by operating as a satellite of the forward Australian dollar-US dollar spot and forward markets and the Asian dollar market? (The Asian dollar market is in US dollar deposits in Singapore.) Its bid rate for euro-Australian dollars would be the return earned from selling Australian dollars spot for US dollars, investing in an Asian dollar deposit (bid-rate) and buying Australian dollars forward for US dollars. Its offer rate for euro- Australian dollars would be the cost of borrowing Asian (offer rate), selling spot for Australian dollars and buying US dollars forward for the maturity of the loan.

The Singapore bank could not act as an agent of the domestic

Australian money market. Restrictions in Australia prevent the free flow of capital. The relation of a euro-Australian dollar market to the domestic market would be similar to that of euro-sterling to domestic sterling. A euro-Australian dollar market could equally be termed a 'free' Australian dollar market in contrast to the controlled domestic market.

In Chapter 1 (p. 21) it was shown that the rate of interest in the 'free' money market of a currency with restricted tradability was likely to be higher than on the domestic where certain credit demands were excluded. Non-residents, foreign exchange speculators and local residents who wish to borrow to finance investment in other currencies and countries are normally denied access to the controlled domestic markets.

Currencies of restricted tradability for which euro-markets are found have typically broad forward markets. In contrast bid-offer spreads on forward Australian-dollars – and other restricted currencies that have failed to develop in euro-form – are wide, indicating market narrowness. Sometimes a forward market is non-existent; then the formation of a satellite euro-market is of course impossible.

When in May 1977 the domestic money market quote for three-months maturity was $10\frac{3}{4}$–11 per cent, that in a hypothetical euro-market would have been $10\frac{3}{4}$–$12\frac{3}{4}$ per cent (based on available forward Australian dollar quotes). The notional 'mid-rates' are $10\frac{7}{8}$ per cent and $11\frac{3}{4}$ per cent respectively. As expected the euro (free) mid-rate is above the domestic. Indicated dealing costs would be so wide in the euro-market however that the gains of freedom would be more than frittered away. A depositor would earn only the same there, $10\frac{3}{4}$ per cent, as in the controlled domestic market.

A potential borrower of Australian dollars, excluded from the domestic market, may prefer to assume an exchange risk and borrow a money with much narrower dealing costs such as US dollars. A non-resident investing in Australia, denied access to the local credit market, would prefer normally to borrow euro-dollars rather than request a Singapore bank to manufacture a euro-Australian dollar loan. He would so avoid being charged the high expenses of market-making in forward Australian dollars.

The Australian dollar is but one example of a 'free' external money market failing to grow. The absence of euro-Swedish, Norwegian kroner could have been used equally as an illustration. The common source of *euro-failure* is that the cost of the 'unnatural' creation of US dollar assets in the essential swap transactions would be greater than any conceivable convenience yield for transactors.

UNEQUAL COMPETITION BETWEEN BANKS

International competition between banks is a reality only in the three major euro-markets – Swiss francs, West German marks and US dollars (the three 'dream' currencies). In the minor euro-markets banks which have an important presence in the country of issue of the currency have a comparative advantage. If seeking a quote on euro-Belgian francs in London, it is best to approach a Belgian bank there; the keenest euro-sterling quotes are found at British banks in Paris. In contrast a bank with no significant representation in the US can produce highly competitive euro-dollar quotes. The explanation of these findings is again to be found in the properties of market-making.

Euro-sterling quotes are generated normally as a satellite of the euro-dollar and spot and forward dollar-pound markets. A non-British bank in Paris will act simply as a broker in the three prime markets. Its procedure is demonstrated in Figure 2.3.

Spot £-$ 1·7204–06
3-month £-$ 207–201 swap
3-month euro-$ 5.625–5·75 % (p.a.)
swap points

$$\text{Bid: } 400 \left[\frac{1·7206 \times 1·0141}{1·7005} - 1 \right] = 10·40\%$$

$$\text{Offer: } 400 \left[\frac{1·7204 \times 1·0144}{1·6997} - 1 \right] = 10.69\%$$

Brokerage   1/16 %
euro-Sterling quote   10·40–10·69 %

FIG. 2.3   Euro-sterling calculation

A British bank in Paris is likely to act in a different way. Its parent in London is a market-maker in forward and spot dollar-pound and euro-dollars. The Paris branch will treat accepting euro-sterling deposit as three inventory entries:
1. a sale of spot dollars for pounds to the client – entered in the bank's spot dollar-pound market-making book,

2. acceptance of a euro-dollar deposit from the client – entered in the euro-dollar deposit book,
3. a forward sale of pounds for dollars to the client – entered in the forward pound-dollar book.

The branch bank's dealing room, together with Head Office, manage each of the three dealing inventories with a measure of interdependence.

At certain times the bank will find excess (positive or negative) inventories building up in one or more of its books and will start its bid-offer quote to attract business in the desired direction. For example it might have an excessive short position in three months forward pounds. The bank may then change its forward sterling quote to 1·7002–1·7005, attracting sellers of forward sterling. It would adjust its euro-sterling quote consistently to 10·30–10·56 per cent thereby enticing borrowers of euro-pounds to its doors.

The example demonstrates that the keenest euro-pound quotes are likely to be made by British banks because they are the major market-makers in the sterling exchange markets. If a non-British bank is approached, it is likely to act as agent with a British bank. The client has to choose between using an agent – with the inherent conflicts of interest which result – or approaching the British banks himself.

The euro-financier-franc market is not a satellite of the foreign exchange markets but of the domestic Belgian money market. No restrictions impede the flow of financier francs from Brussels to London (or in the reverse direction). Narrower quotes can be formed in euro-francs by broking with Brussels than with the foreign exchange and euro-dollar markets. Belgian banks in London will adjust their bid-offer spreads in accordance with whether their parents have excess or deficient inventories in their domestic franc market-making. The most favourable quotes are ultimately to be located therefore with Belgian banks.

The three euro-markets denominated in dream currencies differ essentially from the others. They are prime markets in borrowing and lending deposits. Business is largely between non-residents of the country issuing the currency of denomination. A high proportion of transactors in euro-deutschmarks for example have no direct business association with West Germany.

The three markets are sufficiently broad for banks with no presence in the country of issue to attract sufficient loan and deposit business to be independent market-makers. Swiss, British, West

German and US banks in London can all form independent quotes in euro-dollars, euro-deutschmarks and euro-Swiss francs.

SUPERIOR CREDIT STATUS OF US BANKS

US banks and their subsidiaries do have one major advantage in the euro-dollar market which does not derive from any market-making considerations. The largest US banks have the top credit ratings in the international banking community. This is due first to their superior capital protection and second to a belief in their ultimate access to the Federal Reserve in its role of Lender of Last Resort to the US banking system. These two considerations do not imply that the top American banks form a narrower bid-offer spread in the euro-dollar interbank market: the reverse tends to be true. Superior credit rating permits a lower bid rate, whilst their offer-rate is at the going market rate as most bank borrowers will not have similar top credit status. In the special case where the borrower is another top American bank the offer rate will be reduced. In general though superior credit rating confers the privilege of quoting a wider bid-offer spread.

Differential credit status is well illustrated in the London euro-dollar certificate of deposit (CD) market. Top US banks there can issue negotiable CDs that for three-month maturities yield $\frac{1}{8}$ per cent less than a three-month deposit. A UK or Japanese bank – both in the second tier of the market – would gain no yield advantage from issuing CDs rather than deposits. Their CDs are difficult to trade and buyers will not accept a lower yield.

If CDs are a cheaper form of finance than deposits, why do the top American banks not replace more of their deposit liabilities with CDs? The key to the problem posed is the name consciousness of investors in the CD market. A CD issued by Chase Manhatten is not a perfect substitute for a Citibank CD. Investors want a balanced mix of names in their CD portfolios. If Citibank greatly increased its CD issue at the expense of its deposits, it would have to pay a higher yield on CDs and their comparative cheapness would lessen. The optimum proportion of CDs to issue is that which maximises the *total* cost saving compared to deposits. The CD market can be described technically as one of monopolistic competition.

MONEY MARKET ARBITRAGE BETWEEN LUXEMBOURG AND
FRANKFURT

Arbitrage between a euro-market and the corresponding domestic
market is normally profitable only for banks which are active in
both. German banks for example are best placed to arbitrage
between the euro-deutschmark market centred in Luxembourg and
the domestic deutschmark market in Frankfurt.

To understand the nature of deutschmark money market
arbitrage a knowledge of reserve requirement regulations is needed.
As at summer 1977 resident interbank deposits in Frankfurt were
free of reserve requirements; non-bank deposits placed by both
residents and non-residents were subject to a 10 per cent reserve, as
were interbank deposits placed by banks outside West Germany.
The Bundesbank does not pay interest on these mandatory reserves
placed with itself.

In the context of those reserve requirements consider an arbitrage
situation such as existed on the morning of 17 May 1977. The
opening three-month rate in the Luxembourg interbank euro-
deutschmark market was 3·9–4·1 per cent. In Frankfurt it was 4·4–
4·6 per cent for resident interbank deposits. A bank which was not
itself a market-maker in Frankfurt and Luxembourg would not
have seen a significant arbitrage opportunity. A bank which was a
market-maker in neither centre would have to borrow at the offer
rate of 4·1 per cent in Luxembourg and would receive only 4·0 per
cent (the bid rate for resident deposits less 10 per cent due to cost of
reserve requirement on non-resident deposits) in Frankfurt. The
operation would be at a loss. A bank which was a market-maker in
Luxembourg but not in Frankfurt might attract funds in the former
at the bid rate of 3·9 per cent. But it would get only the bid rate, less
reserve requirement, of 4·0 per cent in Frankfurt. It would do better
to hope to find a taker in Luxembourg at the offer rate there of 4·1
per cent.

Only the bank which is actively market-making both in Luxembourg and Frankfurt can seize an arbitrage opportunity. It can bid
for funds at 3·9 per cent in Luxembourg and hope to find a taker at
the Frankfurt offer rate of 4·6 per cent. Ten per cent of the funds
brought in from Luxembourg must be placed with the Bundesbank
where zero interest is paid. 4·6 per cent is earned on the 90 per cent
remainder making a net total yield of 4·14 per cent. The arbitrage
'turn' made is 0·24 per cent.

The arbitrage operation is not riskless. The borrowing in Luxembourg and lending in Frankfurt do not occur simultaneously. Having been offered a deposit at the bid rate in Luxembourg. The German bank must wait for a borrower to take the funds at the offer rate in Frankfurt. The bank will shade down its Frankfurt offer rate and shade up its Luxembourg bid rate to stimulate arbitrage flows on which to earn profit. Even so some time interval may elapse before the Frankfurt transaction is possible and the rate of interest there could easily have declined a quarter of a point by then. Many banks in the arbitrage business will not consider an operation worthwhile unless the maximum possible profit is at least $\frac{1}{2}$ per cent.

ARBITRAGE BETWEEN FEDERAL FUNDS AND THE OVERNIGHT EURO-DOLLAR MARKET

Federal funds are deposits with the US Federal Reserve Banks. An active overnight market exists in these. The market-makers are the top US banks. No reserve requirements apply to Federal fund borrowings. For similar reasons as those in the deutschmark example, arbitrage opportunities between Federal funds and overnight euro-dollars are available normally only for market-makers in both markets – in practice the large US banks. Arbitrage is limited in time to about two hours due to the time zone difference between the American and European markets.

A technical clearing procedure complicates Federal funds – euro-dollar arbitrage. Euro-dollar business is cleared through a clearing house in New York. To turn funds received in the euro-dollar market into Federal funds takes at least twenty-four hours. In contrast Federal funds are acceptable for same-day settlement in the euro-dollar market.

Suppose therefore that Federal funds rate is $5\frac{3}{8}$–$5\frac{1}{2}$ per cent, and overnight euro-dollar rate is $5\frac{1}{2}$–$5\frac{5}{8}$ per cent. The American bank would hope to attract Federal funds at $5\frac{3}{8}$ per cent and be asked to lend overnight euro-dollars at $5\frac{5}{8}$ per cent. Because of the 24-hour clearance needed the arbitrage transaction has to be spaced over two days. Today it does the euro-dollar loan leg of the transaction at $5\frac{5}{8}$ per cent. Tomorrow it hopes still to bid Federal funds for $5\frac{3}{8}$ per cent, which can be applied that same day to clear its debit balance with the Clearing House. The euro-dollar loan is repaid, but it is not until the following day that payment can be received in Federal funds in New York.

Arbitrage between Federal funds and overnight euro-dollars is inherently risky as a result of having to spread the operation over two days. The rewards are not great. One quarter point margin overnight on $20 m. yields about $175. Sometimes arbitrage will take the simpler form of a US bank deciding passively to have an unbalanced euro-book overnight and borrow Federal funds the following morning in New York to square its position at the Clearing House.

MONEY CANUTISM

Pretensions of sovereignty have become epitomised in the legend of King Canute. The King had his throne placed at the water's edge and ordered the waves to turn back so as not to wet his majestic feet. His successors are not difficult to find in the robes of Ministers of Finance.

The most extreme form of economic canutism is exemplified by finance ministries of very small states. In small, open economies it is conceivable that dealing costs in the forward exchange market of the local currency against the US dollar are less than in the domestic credit market. Exports and imports are a very high proportion of GNP. International trade gives rise to hedging transactions not only of invoices payable and receipts, but also of orders placed. It may be cheaper for domestic money market quotes to be generated as a satellite of the foreign exchange markets and the euro-dollar market than by independent market-making.

The growth of an independent domestic credit market could also be hindered by the high cost of intermediation between borrowers and lenders. Local residents may wish typically to place very short-term deposits and borrow on a long-term basis. Banks would have to charge a higher margin on local currency than dollar lending to justify the risk implicit in greater mismatching of maturities.

One method of reducing intermediation costs would be to deal in dollar swaps. A bank would finance long-term local currency loans by borrowing long-term dollar deposits and by swapping them into the local currency. Short-term local deposits received would be swapped out into short-term dollar deposits. A better match of local currency loan and deposit maturities may thus be obtained by using the forward exchange markets.

The swap operations described would cause the bank to be net long in short-term forward local currency contracts and net short in long-term contracts. The bank's exchange and interest rate exposure would be hedged when spot and forward positions are considered together. Assumption of net speculative positions by non-banks or banks in the forward exchange market is however essential to the intermediation. Speculators in aggregate must have a short position in near-term local currency forward contracts and a long position for longer maturities. The resulting currency straddle between dates is not riskless. Sometimes the central bank may ease strains in the domestic credit market by itself straddling in the forward exchange market, if exacerbated maturity mismatching is the source of present difficulties. The burden of intermediation to be borne by private speculators and its cost is thereby reduced.

The likelihood of the local credit market being a satellite of the foreign exchange and dollar markets is particularly great in a small state that is an offshore financial centre. The problem has become well-known to the monetary authorities in Bahrain and Singapore which are both centres of large and growing offshore dollar markets.

Bahrain has sponsored the growth of an international dollar market since 1975. In principle it should be particularly cheap for local banks to generate Bahraini dinar money market quotes by swapping dollars from the local dollar market into dinars. The rate quoted on a dinar deposit would be the return from selling dinars spot for dollars, investing in a local dollar deposit and buying dinars forward for dollars. The rate should be keener than if the bank made a market independently in dinar deposits waiting to offset a deposit with a dinar loan. The narrowness of the dinar market would necessitate a wider bid-offer spread.

The Bahrain Monetary Authority has resisted the transformation of the domestic dinar money market into a satellite. A number of measures have been introduced to provide shelter from the winds of the international economy. Banks licensed to conduct offshore dollar business in Bahrain are not permitted to deal with residents in the dinar market. The effect is to increase the potential cost of creating dinar deposits by satellite operations. Banks dealing in dinars would not normally have access to the local dollar market and would not therefore be able to complete swap transactions there. The dollar borrowing or lending component of the satellite operation would have to be completed with dollar markets in Europe or Asia. The costs of dealing in dollars with distant centres in different time zones and political jurisdictions is greater. Independent market-making in dinars is thus protected.

The Singapore Monetary Authority has acted similarly to Bahrain in protecting the domestic credit market from satellite competition. Access of local residents to the Asian dollar market is restricted. Quotas are imposed on resident deposits placed there.

MONEY ABSURDITY

If the domestic money market were to become a satellite of the foreign exchange and euro-dollar markets, it is questionable whether the state should continue to issue its own money brand. The exotic nature of the local money would be demonstrated by the realisation that underlying all transactions in it is a dollar borrowing or loan. A swap translates the dollar transaction into local currency denomination. The cost of the translation is visibly the dealing costs associated with the forward and spot exchange transactions. Local residents should find it cheaper to operate in dollars than the local currency. The persistence of the local currency's use would be due to government promotion and institutional considerations.

An analogy to the promotion of a small money brand is official use of an unpopular language. For example when a colony became independent often the official language was changed back to an ancient dialect. In practice the language of commerce remained that of the old imperial power. Translation into the archaic language was costly but necessary for official documentation purposes.

3 Currencies are Commodities in Chicago

The nature of money has been debated with as much fervour by economists as has the nature of God by theologians. Both concepts are abstract. Everyone can identify commodities such as copper, silver, gold, platinum, coffee, cocoa and sugar. We can visualise them in physical form. But what about a US dollar bank deposit? Its possession gives the owner the right to acquire goods. Without the back-up of a legal contract between the depositor and his bank the deposit would be worth no more than the paper on which his account statement is rendered.

Despite its abstract quality the outward forms of money are readily perceptible. Trading currencies shares many characteristics with commodity futures trading. Techniques of investment, speculation and arbitrage in currencies have a counterpart in the commodity futures markets. The trader on the floor of the Chicago Mercantile Exchange has no more awe of dealing in Swiss francs than in pork bellies.

SHORT-SELLING

The scope for short-selling is greater for currencies than for commodities. A commodity's value depends on its physical characteristics whilst a currency's is related to qualities that transcend its physical form. The distinction explains the different possibilities of short-selling.

Many of the holders of a commodity, for example copper, derive a convenience yield from their inventory. By holding copper in a warehouse in Hamburg the German metal merchant is ready to supply random demands for the metal from consumers in the vicinity. He charges a fee for that service. He would be willing to hold some copper in Hamburg even if the expected appreciation in

66

price was less than the inventory's financing and storage cost. He would hope to more than make up the difference from his profits as a metal merchant. They are earned by being able to deliver at short notice copper to specific locations. Carrying an inventory is therefore essential.

Many merchants hedge their inventory by selling the metal forward, say three months, in a commodity futures market in London, Chicago or New York. The covered return from the inventory is the premium of the three-month forward over the spot price less storage and insurance charges. The amount by which that is less than the relevant three-month interest rate is termed 'convenience rent'. The expected yield which the merchant hopes to gain in fees from his marginal inventory should equal the convenience rent.

A physical short-seller of a commodity (copper) operates by borrowing the copper from an inventory holder, selling it spot for currency (dollars) and investing in a dollar deposit. The lender continues to pay storage costs, but to the borrower instead of the warehouseman. Physical short-selling is rare being confined mainly to inter-dealer and certain contrived financial arbitrage transactions.

When the covered return from copper is less than the dollar interest rate profitable arbitrage may be possible. The pure arbitrager would borrow copper, sell it spot, invest in a three-month dollar deposit and buy copper forward three months. The merchant arbitrager sells inventory spot and buys it forward three months. Both types of arbitrage transaction are profitable only if the margin of the covered return below the interest rate is more than the marginal convenience yield. The pure arbitrager would have to pay compensation to the copper lender equal to his expected consequential loss of convenience yield. The merchant arbitrager would have to impute loss of convenience yield against the gross profit from his transaction. Arbitrage ensures therefore only that convenience rent equals marginal convenience yield.

Inventories of some metals are so large that their marginal convenience yield is zero. This has traditionally been so for investment commodities like gold, platinum and silver. Following the 1975 recession and the excess production subsequent to the 1973–4 commodity boom, some base metals – zinc and copper – have become investment metals. Many of the holders of these commodities hold simply warehouse bearer warrants in bank vaults or under the mattress. Unquestionably their marginal convenience yield is zero and arbitrage ensures that the covered return from buying them spot and selling forward equals the corresponding money market interest rate.

The concept of convenience yield is also meaningful for currencies. A US import-export agent derives convenience yield from holding some working balances in deutschmarks if he conducts business regularly with West Germany. Transaction costs of currency exchange are saved. Yet, at the margin, convenience yield on a *freely tradable* currency must be zero. To see this suppose the three-month euro-deutschmark interest rate was below covered parity with euro-dollars. The difference would equal the convenience rent on deutschmarks. The non-zero convenience rate would not persist for long. The arbitrager would issue three-month deutschmark paper (equivalently borrow three-month deutschmarks), sell the deutschmarks, so raised spot for dollar, invest in a three-month euro-dollar deposit and buy deutschmarks three months forward.

An equivalent type of paper transaction was not possible in the copper example. There the arbitrager has to borrow physical copper from a present holder. It is true that he could issue 'copper paper', promising to pay the bearer the value of say 25 tons of copper in three month's time. Unlike the deutschmark example copper paper would not be a perfect substitute for physical copper in existence. A claim indexed to the copper price does not provide any convenience yield to its bearer. He cannot use it to deliver metal to a client. In contrast any deutschmark paper can be used, directly or indirectly, to satisfy a deutschmark debt.

CONVENIENCE RENT ON RESTRICTED CURRENCIES

Freely tradable currencies were chosen on purpose in the above example. The arbitrage transaction essential to the elimination of convenience rent cannot often occur with restricted currencies. Their interest ràtes were demonstrated in Chapter 1 to be often domestically below covered parity with freely tradable currencies. Exchange controls prevent the physical short-selling of restricted currencies. If the three-month domestic French franc rate is 8 per cent, and the three-month euro-franc rate 10 per cent, a 2 per cent convenience rate is being charged effectively on domestic franc holdings. A non-resident of France who holds francs with a Paris bank should derive transaction cost savings of at least 2 per cent compared to the alternative of holding francs with a London bank.

The concept of convenience yield helps to provide an insight into the exchange rate implications of a deposit switch from the domestic to euro-currency market. Domestic and euro-sterling, where the differential between the two markets has sometimes been as much as 5 per cent on three-month deposits is used as the example.

Suppose a backwoods non-resident holder of domestic sterling becomes aware of the existence of the euro-sterling market and realises further that he is deriving no convenience yield. Yet he wishes to maintain a sterling exposure and so transfers the sterling to a bank in Paris where he has been quoted a much keener deposit rate than in London. What is the effect on the pound-dollar exchange rate?

In aggregate there must correspond an equal flow from euro-pound to domestic pound to accommodate our backwoodsman. Someone must be tempted to pull pounds in from Paris to London. The mechanism is a narrowing of the euro-pound, domestic-pound interest rate differential, so decreasing convenience rent on London pounds. Some holders of Paris pounds expect sufficient convenience yield from London pounds to now justify holding the latter in preference at the lower convenience rent. The interest rate adjustment occurs on euro-pounds being the much narrower market.

Euro-pound rates are at covered parity with euro-dollars. The euro-pound rate decline requires a narrowing of the forward discount on pounds. This can be matched either by a fall in the spot exchange rate or a rise in the forward rate. In practice the spot rate will bear the brunt of the adjustment.

The euro-pound market is largely a satellite of the euro-dollar and dollar-pound exchange market as was discussed in Chapter 2 (p. 46). On receiving the euro-pound deposit from the backwoodsman the Paris bank sells the pounds spot for dollars, buys pounds forward and places the dollars in the euro-dollar market. Speculators in the forward pound-dollar market will supply the forward pounds for a small movement in the forward pound-dollar exchange rate. Speculators are sometimes rare however in the spot dollar-pound exchange market. Who is going to sell dollars for spot pounds when the interest rate on domestic pounds is lower than on euro-pounds? Investment in euro-pounds is fundamentally a purchase of forward pounds plus an investment in euro-dollars. The only purchaser (net) of spot pounds can be someone who can justify holding it at the now lower convenience rent – someone who derives convenience yield from London pound balances.

The spot speculator is in shorter supply than his forward counterpart because he must also have a working need for pounds. The narrowing of the convenience rent is effected primarily by movement of the spot exchange rate since speculators are less ready to absorb excess pound supplies in the spot than forward market.

The final outcome is that the London pound deposit sold by the backwoodsman is purchased by someone who earns convenience yield equal to the lower euro-pound, domestic-pound interest rate differential. Corresponding to the new euro-pound deposit of the backwoodsman is a forward sale of pounds plus an investment in euro-dollars (the satellite set of transactions undertaken by the Paris bank to manufacture the euro-pound deposit). There has occurred in aggregate a reverse flow from euro-pounds into domestic pounds equal to the original outflow.

WHEN DOLLARS BECOME EURO-DOLLARS

The transfer of deposits from the domestic to euro-market has no significant exchange rate implications for freely tradable currencies. Suppose there is a flow of dollars from the domestic US money market to the euro-dollar market as US corporations become aware of the greater competitiveness of rates there. The euro-dollar market is a prime one. Its market-makers react to the increased source of deposits by lowering both their bid and offer quotes. The interest rate differential between domestic and euro-dollar deposits narrows.

US reserve requirements which apply to most deposits (with the exception of Federal funds) prevent the equalising of deposit rates for non-bank clients between the US and Europe. Arbitrage by non-bank borrowers is not impeded. A dollar is a dollar whether borrowed in the US or euro-market.

If borrower arbitrage were perfect, bank loan costs on dollars would be the same on both sides of the Atlantic. No change would occur in dollar interest rates in Europe or the US as a result of the transfer of funds between the two. A shrinkage of bank assets and liabilities in the US would be matched by an increase in Europe, measured in constant purchasing-power dollars. The real exchange rate of the dollar would be unaltered. The outcome in nominal dollar terms would depend on whether the Federal Reserve adapted its high-powered money supply policy.

Borrower arbitrage is not in practice perfect. The inflow of US funds into the euro-dollar market would tend to depress interest rates there relative to those in the US. A small amount of the extra dollars deposited in Europe would be borrowed by non-US residents, tempted by their lowered cost, to finance the purchase of non-dollar assets. A small real exchange rate change results.

A similar analysis would show that switching between domestic and euro-deutschmarks does not significantly affect the deutschmark's real exchange rate. The euro- and domestic deutschmark markets are highly integrated for non-bank borrowers. Non-integration was the key to the different real exchange rate implication of flows between euro- and domestic pounds. Exchange restrictions drive a wedge between borrowing costs in the two markets by preventing many borrowers from arbitraging.

The differing exchange rate implications of switching from restricted and freely tradable currencies are in part intuitive. When a depositor switches pounds from London to Paris funds are being transferred from the controlled to the 'free' sterling market. An exchange rate fall accommodates the capital outflow by generating a trade surplus to match it. As the trade surplus is realized the speculators who purchased the pounds sold by the backwoodsman themselves liquidate their new pound position. The pounds withdrawn to Paris are matched eventually by a reduction of loans to UK residents. In contrast the transfer of funds from the US to the euro-dollar system was motivated by the latter's greater efficiency in intermediating between borrowers and lenders. The outcome is a transfer of intermediation function from the US to euro-banks, but no net capital outflow.

BORROWERS CONVENIENCE YIELD

The convenience yield so far discussed has been for the depositor. Free tradability ensured that depositors' convenience yield tended to zero at the margin. No such condition applies to borrowers' convenience yield which can remain positive.

Convenience yield on borrowing a currency, for example Canadian dollars, derives from hedging demand. A Canadian businessman may prefer to borrow Canadian dollars to finance his enterprise even though the Canadian dollar interest rate superiority over the US dollar interest rate is more than the expected depreciation of the Canadian against the US currency. A large proportion of the businessman's cash flow may be denominated in Canadian dollars and to borrow US dollars would cause a mismatch.

Convenience yield on deposits may decline more sharply than on borrowings. Yet in equilibrium the marginal convenience yield on Canadian dollar deposits must be zero since the Canadian dollar is freely tradable. Consistent with zero convenience rent on deposits is a continued positive marginal convenience yield to borrowers. That relation would be supported by a finding that the Canadian dollar yielded a more superior return adjusted for exchange rate changes than the US dollar. The higher real yield on Canadian dollars than US dollars would be compensation for the marginal holder accepting denomination of his deposit in a less popular brand of dollar.

SWISS BANKERS AND GOLD

A large proportion of holders of both Swiss francs and gold derive no convenience yield from their investment. Such pure investors in gold and Swiss francs intend to include them as permanent components of their investment portfolio. Pure investment demand is more shiftable than transactions balance or merchanting demand. Swings in excess demand for Swiss francs and gold are therefore likely to be particularly significant.

The speculator in gold or Swiss francs recognises the importance of potential shifts in their pure investment appeal. Real cost considerations – changing gold mine technology, Switzerland's balance of trade – are of minor importance in the determination of the gold price or the Swiss franc real exchange rate. The speculator, in contrast to the pure investor, does not consider either gold or the franc as permanent additions to his portfolio.

Swiss bankers advise their private clients to hold certain proportions of their portfolio in gold and Swiss francs. They are the unshakable rocks that in a world of catastrophe are most likely to retain their value. Popularity of each changes. Some banks in 1976 advised clients to hold as little as 5 per cent in gold, compared to 20 per cent two years before. The successful speculator would have forecast that shift in pure investment demand.

Investment holdings of gold have been estimated at seventy years production of the metal. A 10 per cent shift in investment demand has much greater implications for the gold price than any conceivable change in demand by industrial users or jewellers who derive convenience yield. Similarly probable shifts in net investment demand for Swiss francs far outweigh likely net trade flows in or out of Switzerland. Trying to predict the Swiss franc's real exchange rate by examining Swiss export prospects, including the plight of the cuckoo clock and watch industries, would be as absurd as predicting the gold price by examining changes in mining costs and demand for jewellery.

Shifts in net investment demand for gold can be expected to be more volatile than for Swiss francs. It was analysed in Chapter 1 (p. 9) how both some borrowers and some lenders 'dream' in Swiss francs. There is a dreamer element in the borrowing demand for francs. A decline in dreamer investment demand for francs will often be matched by a decreased borrowing demand. An event which decreases the popularity of the franc for investors will often have a parallel effect on borrowers. For example for three months following the Credit Suisse Chiasso revelations in the spring of 1977 both borrowing and lending of Swiss francs by non-residents decreased sharply. Both borrowers and lenders shied away from currency uncertainty.

Physical short-selling of gold is uncommon. In no way is gold now used to denominate borrowings. A shift in popularity will affect investment demand for the metal and there will be no offsetting borrowing influence. It is therefore apparent that investment taste changes are a source of greater volatility in the price of gold than of Swiss francs. The non-use of gold as a unit of account in private loan contracts is a symptom of its essential non-monetary nature.

BID-OFFER SPREADS

The bid-offer spread on forward exchange transactions is greater than on spot. For example on Friday, 22 June 1977 the opening dollar-deutschmark quote was 2·2620–2·2630 DM/$ spot and 2·2500–2·2520 for three-month delivery. Forward currency markets are thinner than spot and market-makers there charge a wider spread to cover costs of slower turnover inventory. The wider forward spreads have implications for the choice of least cost vehicle for foreign exchange speculation by banks.

The exchange rate exposure gained by assuming a forward exchange position is identical to a borrow-and-lend transaction plus a spot exchange deal. Buying three-month deutschmarks forward for dollars is equivalent to borrowing three-month euro-dollars, selling spot for deutschmarks and investing in a three-month euro-deutschmark deposit. The forward market for three-month dollar-deutschmarks can support independent market-making. It is therefore cheaper to complete a forward deal than undertake the set of equivalent transactions one-by-one. However if one of the component transactions has already been completed in another connection, the forward route to exchange exposure is normally expensive.

Consider an investor with a dollar deposit maturing today who wishes now to assume deutschmark exposure. He will find it cheaper to sell the dollars spot for deutschmarks and invest in a euro-deutschmark deposit than to roll over the dollar deposit and buy deutschmarks forward for dollars. The latter alternative, when broken into its component transactions, involves borrowing and lending dollars and paying two market-making fees to do so. Similarly a bank which wants to assume a long deutschmark exposure, yet not expand its total liabilities, will find it cheaper to purchase a deutschmark deposit with dollars on hand than completing a forward deal.

The same order of costs does not apply to currencies with restricted tradability. Where those currencies are found in euro-form they are satellites of the foreign exchange market and euro-dollar market (see Chapter 2, p. 46). If a Brussels bank is asked to quote for a euro-French franc deposit, it calculates a rate based on what can be earned from selling the francs spot for dollars, placing the dollars in a euro-dollar deposit and buying francs forward for dollars. The bid-offer spread on euro-francs is thus identical to the difference between the bid and offer dollar-franc swap points. Transaction costs cannot therefore be saved by investing in euro-francs rather than purchasing francs forward. The euro-franc deposit is itself a product of a forward franc deal. Even so many investors and borrowers prefer to complete a single transaction in a euro-currency rather than in two currencies separately. The euro-markets in restricted currencies cater for them.

The transactor in a euro-restricted currency should sometimes obtain the keenest deposit quote if he makes payment in US dollars. In the euro-franc example if dollars are presented, the bank does not effect a spot-and-forward exchange which may be expensive. It purchases francs forward which are delivered on maturity to the depositor. The dollars are lent in the euro-dollar market.

In practice banks taking strategic open foreign exchange positions in US dollars, West German marks, Swiss francs and Dutch guilders will do so in the euro-deposit markets. All four are either prime or associate markets. If the bank has investment funds available, transaction costs of purchasing deposits are less than of forward exchange transactions. Open positions in French francs, British pounds, Spanish peseta and Italian lire and others are most cheaply assumed in the forward exchange markets.

COMMODITY FUTURES

The commodity futures markets can be analysed as a solar system similar in many respects to the money market system. The outlines were drawn in Table 2.3. To understand the examples given a brief synopsis is given of the copper futures market.

Copper is traded on the London Metal Exchange (LME) and the New York Commodity Exchange (Comex). In the spot markets bearer warrants are purchased and sold. The warrants entitle the holder to given weights of copper in warehouses approved by the relevant metal exchange. The bearer must pay rent on the copper so held. Warrants traded in New York are drawn on US warehouses. Those traded on the LME are drawn on warehouses in Europe. An LME warrant may not normally be used to satisfy delivery against a New York futures contract or conversely. In London contracts are denominated in pounds: in New York they are in dollars. Market-makers function in London and New York in spot and forward markets.

Though the pound is the currency used to denominate LME copper contracts, speculators calculate normally first what they expect the future spot dollar price of copper will be. Then they make a pure currency judgment of the future spot dollar-pound exchange rate. In general no correlation exists between the dollar-pound rate and the dollar copper price. A depreciation of the pound does not in itself alter the dollar quote of copper. The world demand, measured in dollars, for the metal is not affected significantly by UK currency developments. Asymmetrically the pound copper price is highly dependent on the dollar-pound rate.

A similar two-stage judgment is made in trading Swiss francs. Movement of the Swiss franc-West German mark exchange rate is not correlated with the deutschmark-dollar rate. Germany is Switzerland's largest trading partner and the Swiss balance of trade is most sensitive to the deutschmark-franc exchange rate. In contrast, the deutschmark's relation to the franc is not of great significance in determining the German trade balance. Furthermore investor taste tends to swing between dollars on the one hand and Swiss francs together with deutschmarks on the other.

A speculator in Swiss francs will normally first take a view on its likely movement relative to the deutschmark, analogously to the LME speculator first judging the future dollar copper price. He will trade Swiss francs against dollars because independent market-making does not exist in the franc-mark exchange market. If the speculator wishes to avoid forming a separate judgment of rate movements in the much larger dollar-deutschmark market, he must take an offsetting dollar-deutschmark position. His profit then depends solely on the relative movement of the deutschmark-Swiss franc exchange rate. Although the economics of market-making necessitate all exchange transactions being against the dollar, all currency speculation does not include the dollar as a subject.

Some traders on the LME do not want to be bothered with exposure to the pound exchange risk, similarly to the deutschmark-Swiss franc speculator eschewing a dollar position. Yet the metal dealer may prefer to deal in London to New York where dollar copper contracts are traded. He may contemplate ultimate delivery of a European warrant.

If a sufficient number of copper traders wanted to deal in London dollar copper contracts, the LME could support independent market-making in them. In practice potential LME dollar copper business seems thin. Dealers will, if requested, quote in dollars but only on a satellite basis. They will act as brokers with a bank to obtain the cost of forward pound-dollar cover which they will add to their pound copper quote. The bid-offer spread on the London dollar copper quote is the addition of that on pound copper plus forward pound-dollars plus a brokerage fee. The LME dollar copper market is satellite to the forward exchange and pound copper markets.

The transaction cost of dealing in dollar copper should in principle be greater on the LME than Comex. There two deals together with their bid-offer spreads do not have to be added. If a trader in dollar copper has no reason to be concerned about delivery of a European warrant, he should deal in New York rather than London. If choosing London, he would obtain keener terms by packaging his own dollar-copper contract. He should approach independently market-makers in pound-LME copper and forward pound-dollars and combine for himself the keenest quotes. If he deals simply with a metal dealer, he is trusting that the best forward pound-dollar quote will be obtained.

FINANCIAL ARBITRAGE IN COPPER

Financial arbitrage is common on the LME. Financial institutions and individuals with liquid funds buy copper spot and simultaneously sell it forward three months. Net of storage and insurance costs they earn typically a small margin over the three-month domestic interbank sterling interest rate. The operation is termed in LME language as 'borrowing copper'. 'Lending copper' describes the selling of copper spot and simultaneously buying it forward. Lending is undertaken predominantly by copper merchants reducing temporary excess inventories or investors wishing to realize cash.

There is independent market-making in borrowing and lending copper. For five minutes, twice a day, some LME members concentrate on that type of business. Clients instruct their brokers to execute their orders at those times. By concentrating borrowing and lending business into two fixed sessions it becomes sufficiently thick to support market-makers. The same technique of concentration is used in some small currency markets.

Dealing spreads of financial arbitrage transactions in copper are substantially less than if spot and forward deals were completed separately. The counterpart of market-making in borrowing and lending copper in the currency markets is market-making in combined spot-and-forward exchange transactions. Financial arbitrage in metals can also occur outside the two five minute sessions. Borrowing and lending operations are then satellite to the spot and forward markets and the transaction costs greater. In the currency markets, by contrast, many banks market-make throughout the day in spot-and-forward exchange transactions.

THROUGH THE LOOKING GLASS

Cocteau's film of the Orpheus myth illustrates well a feature of certain satellite market transactions. Death drags her victims through a mirror into the endless passages of the underworld. Sometimes the victim manages to escape by returning through the mirror into the living world. But he is worn by his travels and – intangible to humans – can vanish from their sight when he so wishes.

Sometimes the grip of government controls on market activity can be escaped by penetrating the mirror and returning *à l'Orphée*. The investor, prevented from dealing any longer in a particular prime market, effects a series of transactions in others. He hopes so to return to the initial market producing its commodity as a satellite of markets in which he can deal freely. Neither tax nor control authorities can register fantasy form. The set of satellite transactions are treated individually rather than as a whole.

Consider a non-resident of Switzerland who buys Swiss francs at a Swiss bank. He cannot continue to hold Swiss francs on deposit there without becoming subject to Swiss withholding tax and negative interest penalties. So what does he do? He penetrates the mirror. He sells his Swiss francs for gold. Still in the underworld he sells the gold forward to the Swiss bank. The contract is denominated in Swiss francs. The bank forms the Swiss franc gold quote by offsetting a position in the dollar gold futures market with a forward dollar-Swiss franc deal. That is executed by a bank subsidiary outside Switzerland to avoid National Bank limitations on forward franc positions. The spot purchase and forward sale of gold for Swiss francs is equivalent to a Swiss franc deposit.

By a series of operations the investor has returned through the mirror; he has obtained a Swiss franc deposit in Switzerland as a satellite of the spot gold market, the gold futures market and the forward franc-dollar market. He is the worse for travelling having incurred three sets of bid-offer spreads to return to holding Swiss francs. They are invisible to the Swiss tax or control authorities who register only two gold contracts. His Swiss franc position has been created by agents of the underworld. In the live world of finance they would have been smothered by competition from independent market-makers who could produce Swiss francs much more cheaply than the satellite commodity market operation. The birth of a prime market heralds the death of satellite formations.

US tax attorneys have devised an ingenious method of producing a dollar deposit as a satellite of LME spot and forward silver and the forward pound-dollar market. The Internal Revenue Service (IRS) do not identify the set of transactions as a whole, but each individually. More favourable tax treatment is hence obtained.

A US film-star with high personal earned income borrows $500,000. She sells the dollars for pounds and buys silver on the LME. She simultaneously sells LME silver forward twelve months and the covered return approximates the twelve-month sterling interbank rate. The exchange risk is hedged by selling pounds forward twelve months for dollars, equal to the maturity value of the silver contract. The currency and silver risks are covered and the film-star has the equivalent of a twelve-month dollar deposit.

Interest on the loan of $500,000 can be offset against personal income on which high rates of tax are payable. Profit on the covered sale of silver is treated as capital gain which is taxable at a lower rate. The film-star has so succeeded in transforming high taxed income into low taxed capital gain. Agents' fees and market-makers' spreads are incurred in reproducing the dollar deposit in phantom form.

PHANTOM BORROWING INVISIBLE TO CURRENCY REGULATORS

Only in sinister totalitarian regimes can man's free spirit be suppressed. When a government operating under a liberal constitution prohibits an economic activity, it realises that prohibition is a fiction. It hopes at most to have increased the transaction costs for those engaged in the disliked activity.

An illustration can be drawn from the Bundesbank's attempt at preventing German residents from borrowing money abroad to bring into Germany. The purpose of the controls, abandoned in 1974, was to stave off an appreciation of the deutschmark.

At times the three-month euro-deutschmark rate in Luxembourg and London was 5 per cent and more below Frankfurt money rates. The differential could not be simply arbitraged away because switching euro-deutschmarks into domestic deutschmarks was prohibited. How could an enterprising German have profited from a situation as described?

He would approach a metal dealer in Frankfurt or Zurich. Dealers hold LME warrants on behalf of clients who are investing in metals. The German would negotiate to borrow warrants from the dealer undertaking to re-deliver them within say three months. He places bearer securities as collateral for the warrant loan, or arranges a bank guarantee. The German then sells the warrants, say silver, on the LME for pounds which he sells spot for deutschmarks and invests in the Frankfurt money market. He simultaneously buys silver forward three months on a deutschmark-denominated contract. The LME broker manufactures the deutschmark contract for the German by himself buying an ordinary LME three-month pound silver contract and simultaneously selling deutschmarks three-month forward for pounds. The premium of the three-month pound silver price over the spot approximates the three-month pound interest rate. By borrowing silver warrants and buying them back forward for deutschmarks, the German has effectively borrowed deutschmarks at near the three-month euro-deutschmark rate. (The three-month pound interest rate minus the three-month premium on forward deutschmarks tends to equal the three-month euro-deutschmark rate.)

The German has manufactured euro-deutschmarks as a satellite of the spot and forward silver markets. Borrowing these phantom euro-deutschmarks is not registered by the Bundesbank control authorities. Transaction costs involved are high. The metal broker in Zurich or Frankfurt must be paid a fee for lending warrants (may be as much as 1 per cent per annum). The London broker earns commission for manufacturing a forward deutschmark denominated silver contract. A sequence of bid-offer spreads is further incurred in the spot deutschmark-pound, spot silver and forward silver markets. Even so as much as a 4 per cent turn, net of transaction costs, could have been earned sometimes in 1973 by completing the set of transactions described.

CHICAGO'S INTERNATIONAL MONETARY MARKET

Until the International Monetary Market (IMM) was opened on 16 May 1972 in Chicago currency trading differed in organisation from commodities. Almost all foreign exchange dealing was done by banks who acted as brokers for clients and as market-makers. Commodities by contrast are traded in organised futures exchanges and are bought and sold by open auction. The differing forms have significance not only for competition in brokerage and market-making but also for market efficiency.

The breakdown of fixed exchange rates in 1971 and the dawn of the floating exchange rate era have increased the need for currency speculators. It is they, instead of central banks, who must now absorb excess supplies of currency and short-sell it when excess demand exists. The growth of the IMM has been based on the pioneering of a new foreign exchange dealing technology. It is particularly suited to smaller transactions, including the type of speculative position that it is likely would be assumed by wealthy private investors. Their potential importance as speculators stems from an ability to assume venturesome positions free of the political constraints of the larger corporations.

IMM ORGANISATION

The IMM is a division of Chicago's Mercantile Exchange (CME). They both share the same trading floor. Hogs and pork bellies trade alongside the Swiss franc and the West German mark. When trading is light in commodities, CME members may stray over into the currency sector to transact there. Although CME members may trade on the IMM, the converse is not true.

The IMM trades currency futures contracts. They have standardised delivery dates – the third Wednesday of March, June, September and December. The advantage of standardised delivery dates is to provide market depth and hence narrow bid-offer spreads. When the Exchange was first opened contracts were written for standard dates at only monthly intervals apart but business was found to be too thin. As in the interbank market, turnover in the shorter maturities is highest.

Every futures contract is made with the IMM Clearing House and credit risk is therefore uniform. Members of the Exchange must place margins with the Clearing House, calculated as a fixed percentage of the value of their outstanding contracts. Clients must in turn deposit margins with the members through whom they execute orders. The IMM guarantees all contracts; the possibility of default is almost zero because it insists that members start each day without debt to itself.

An attraction of the IMM is its secondary market facilities. Suppose a trader has a long position in June Swiss francs. To close his position he simply sells a June Swiss franc contract. Unlike in the bank forward exchange market, he is paid the profit by (or pays the loss to) the Clearing House on the same day as closure. Indeed profits and losses are payable daily whether or not realized. After trading hours the Clearing House calculates unrealized losses and gains on all outstanding contracts; margins must be topped up by losers and gains are paid out to the fortunate.

Secondary market trading is easier on the IMM in two further respects. There is no problem of odd maturity dates. Suppose the trader in Swiss francs had instead of dealing on the IMM bought Swiss francs three-months forward for delivery on say August 13 from a New York bank. On 1 July he wishes to close his franc position. He would have to sell francs forward for 13 August. The bid-offer spread will however be wider on a broken month maturity – one and a half months – than on an unbroken one. Further if the deal is completed with a bank other than the original, he has not closed his position entirely. He is still exposed to default risk. One of the banks might go bankrupt before maturity and he would have to honour the contract with the surviving one. The trader is hence in part a captive of the bank with which he made the original contract.

Eight currencies are traded presently on the IMM – the British pound, Canadian dollar, Dutch guilder, West German mark, Japanese yen, Mexican peso, Swiss franc and French franc. The Italian lira was traded from 1972–3, but was delisted because of insufficient interest. The two most popular European currency contracts are the Swiss franc and West German mark. They are two of the three major world investment currencies and broad interest in trading them on the IMM is natural. The Canadian dollar, Mexican peso and Japanese yen contracts enjoy custom from North American trade interests.

The French franc and Dutch guilder markets in the IMM are narrow and function as satellites of the interbank market. A member quoting for a contract in either currency will offset immediately his position with a bank. The bid-offer spread that would justify him making a market in IMM contracts is too broad relative to the quotes he can manufacture as a bank agent. Some traders may prefer to buy and sell IMM francs and guilders to interbank because of the secondary market facilities of the IMM. They will not enjoy the maturity advantage as members will pass on the extra costs of odd-month dates in their satellite deal. The credit mismatching problem of closing positions in the bank forward market are avoided. The IMM provides effectively the facility of shifting the mismatch problem on to the member by the trader.

The IMM represents a technological innovation designed to reduce the costs of small trades. The size of a unit contract in each currency are British £25,000; C$100,000; Peso 1,000,000; Swiss francs 125,000; French francs 125,000; guilder 125,000; DM 125,000; yen 12,500,000. The standardisation of contract sizes and maturity dates allows the IMM market-maker to economise on inventory for a given foreign exchange turnover. He is able thus to reduce bid-offer spreads below what a bank would have to charge on such small transactions. The IMM is not designed to accommodate multi-million dollar deals. If an IMM member was asked to quote on DM 10m, he would immediately offset it in the bank market. He would be operating then as a bank agent.

ARBITRAGE

Arbitrage between the IMM and interbank currency markets is crucial for Chicago's success. Arbitrage increases as a percentage of IMM turnover when trading in a particular currency is light or predominantly in one direction. Members then tend to switch to offsetting deals with banks rather than risk excess build-up of their own inventory. The significance of the proportion of arbitrage business with the interbank market for the IMM is similar to that of business with outside banks for a financial centre or swap business in a euro-currency market. The degree of dependence of a market on arbitrage transactions is a measure of its primeness.

The depth of the IMM would be greatly increased if it gained associate status with the interbank market. Banks themselves would seek quotes on the IMM and deal there if cheaper. On occassions a bank should be able to quote keener terms to a customer as an agent of the IMM than as an independent market-maker. Banks have been reluctant to use the IMM as suggested. They consider it as a rival for their foreign exchange business.

If banks became members of the IMM, arbitrage between the IMM and interbank market would be more efficient. A bank, as market-maker in both markets, would be able to arbitrage profitably when others could not.

Suppose the deutschmark was quoted at 2·2533–43/dollar on the

IMM and at 2·2535–45/dollar for similar size deals in the interbank market. A market-maker in both markets would hope to be offered dollars for 2·2533 in the IMM and find takers at 2·2545 in the interbank market. He would shade slightly his quotes in each place to generate the desired flows.

In practice no IMM market-makers perform that function also in the interbank market. If offered dollars in the IMM for deutschmark at 2·2533/dollar, he would do better by holding the dollars in inventory and hoping for a taker at 2·2543/dollar then selling them immediately in the interbank market at 2·2535/dollar. He would prefer to lower substantially his offer price for deutschmarks to 2·2535 than offload excess dollar inventory in the rival interbank market. The argument is identical to that in Chapter 2 (p. 61) where it was argued that arbitrage between Luxembourg and Frankfurt in deutschmarks was most profitable for German banks with operations in both places.

The IMM Clearing House has done much to encourage arbitrage business, realising its vital role. It has instituted a Class B member category whose activities are confined to arbitrage and therefore exempted from margin requirements. By 1977 no large US banks were Class B members.

IMM HANDICAP

The IMM carries over a handicap from commodity market organisation on which it is based. Daily limits are imposed on the amount by which a currency price can move. When the limit is reached trading stops. If on two successive days the price reaches the limit moving in the same direction, an expanded daily price limit schedule goes into effect. If the price settles at its expanded daily limit on the fourth day, there will be no daily price limit on the fifth day. On the sixth day the normal daily price limit is reinstated.

Despite the genesis tone of these margin provisions, by 1977 they had been activated only once – during the Mexican peso collapse of end-1976. Limits are defended strongly by IMM members. In a crisis they allow more time to raise cash to meet margin requirements than if the quoted price on the exchange moved immediately to its new level. Traders may however be deterred from using the IMM by its limit rules. If they want to lock in a profit subsequent to a large price movement – and the limit rule bars trade on the

IMM – they must close their position on the rival bank market.

Suppose a trader had wanted to realize his profit on a short position in December 1976 in pesos on a day when the limit rule closed the IMM peso market. He would have had to buy forward December pesos in the interbank market. When dealings resumed in IMM pesos he would then have sold forward December pesos in the bank market and closed his position on the IMM. Alternatively he might have let both the IMM and bank contracts run to maturity. The pesos delivered against the bank contract would be used to meet the IMM delivery requirements. Whichever procedure is followed extra transactional costs are incurred.

The IMM differs from the interbank market by providing for separation of brokerage and dealing function. Members are not permitted to trade with their clients. Their orders must be executed with other market-makers. When a trader places an order with a member he can be reasonably sure that the member will seek quotes from many market-makers and select the keenest. None of the market-makers approached are concerned with the credit status of the broker's client. All contracts are effectively guaranteed by the Clearing House.

In the interbank market, unlike on the IMM, market-makers will not quote without the credit status and often name of the transactor being revealed. The market-maker's contract is made directly with the ultimate client so that credit information is essential. Smaller clients, who do not have a recognised credit status, will find it difficult to find realistic quotes other than from their own bank which has knowledge of their affairs. They do not in consequence have access to competitive market-making.

Large currency-traders, although they are well placed to seek competitive quotes, may not wish to reveal their identity to many market-makers. A corporate or agency name may carry significance in the market, being associated with possession of special knowledge, and move the price. If for example it became widely known that IBM was selling Canadian dollars forward to hedge Canadian assets, other corporations may be motivated to act similarly. The IMM separation of brokerage and market-making function is thus seen as advantageous by both large and small transactors. It has been rumoured that even some minor central banks and large OPEC investors prefer the anonymity of the IMM to the more personalised bank market.

SOFT MONEY AND HARD COMMODITIES

It was shown in Chapter 1 (p. 19) that the rate of return on restricted currencies was likely to be below that on freely tradable ones. The expected rate of return on most forms of investment in the country applying capital export controls will be inferior to that in countries which permit free movement of capital. Acquisition of investment commodities is an exception.

Large excess inventories relative to commercial needs characterise investment commodities and the marginal convenience yield on them is zero. Their ranks are swelled during a recessionary period. Inventories then build up because of an over-expansion of mining capacity during the previous period of boom. Thus the convenience rent on copper fell to zero in the 1975 recession and has not yet again become positive.

The price of an investment commodity is almost identical all over the world because shipping costs per unit value are very low. Storage costs are small. The current price must be sufficiently low to provide investors with an expected capital gain equal to storage and financing costs plus an appropriate risk premium. The expected capital gain must be competitive with alternative investments for residents of countries which permit free trade in capital. They are the main investors in metals. When residents of other countries buy investment commodities they are buying assets whose prices are determined competitively with others sold in free capital markets. Hence follows their attractiveness relative to those whose prices are determined in the controlled domestic market.

Investment in metals–silver, copper, gold and platinum–is risky. Residents of restricted currency countries will hold them in greater proportion to their wealth, but they will still represent only a small part.

ENERGY MONEY INVESTORS NOT SO LUCKY

It was discussed in Chapter 1 how normally interest rates in countries benefiting from growing energy revenues would be well below the domestic rate of inflation. The discrepancy is due to the rate of currency depreciation being less externally than internally. In that context investment in metals is not likely to yield a positve real return. The divergence between external and internal depreciation reflects an increasing relative price of non-traded goods in terms of traded goods.

Surely investment in non-traded goods inventory would produce a positive real return for residents of the energy money state? But the ratio of value to unit weight and volume is usually less for non-traded than traded goods. Storage costs are hence much higher than for traded goods. Further non-traded goods are generally less standardised and subject to higher risk of obsolescence. The combined storage and obsolescence costs on non-traded goods inventory are normally greater than the differential rate of external and internal fall in currency value.

It may be thought that income-yielding non-traded goods, real estate in particular, are attractive investments in an energy money economy. Maintenance and obsolescence costs can be provided out of rental income. The building's value in the long run moves with replacement cost (less obsolescence) which tends to move consistently with an index of non-traded goods prices. The special properties of real estate investment are however well-known. As soon as residents become aware of the metamorphosis of their currency into an energy money they rush to buy buildings and land. Their prices will be bid well above replacement cost so as to bring their expected rate of return into equilibrium with the now lower interest rate.

As a result of building values shooting above present replacement cost, a construction boom is generated. The supply of new buildings eventually slows down the rise of rents and values. The boom causes the cost of building to increase as resources are scarce – especially land. These developments accommodate a rate of inflation of real estate values less than that of the general consumer price index. At first values overshoot replacement cost. Then the rate of increase in replacement cost is slowed down due to the longer-term easing of pressure on short-term supplies to the construction industry.

Energy money investors are condemned to a lower real rate of return on capital due to their currency's exchange rate behaviour. The more than compensating benefits are received as windfall capital gains by lucky investors at the time of energy discovery.

Intense real estate investment is a feature of energy rich monies. The reverse is true of countries suffering from sustained capital flight. External depreciation is there greater than internal. Non-traded goods prices increase less than the general price index and real estate investment is relatively unattractive.

Laboratory tests of financial theories are hard to devise. Superficial evidence would support the hypothesised patterns of real estate investment. A fantastic building boom has occurred in OPEC countries since the quadrupling of the oil price in 1973. In countries such as Italy and Mexico that have suffered from capital haemorrhages commercial real estate development has halted.

HARD MONEY INDEXATION

Restricted currencies are uncompetitive with those freely traded. Not only are their rates of return lower, but also their internal and external purchasing power tends to depreciate more unpredictably. Though regulations prevent the using of foreign currencies for internal transactions, they do not prevent their use as unit of account. In Italy for example there have been some issues of dollar-indexed bonds which are subscribed for and payable in lire. When an Italian purchases dollar-indexed paper no net capital outflow results. The rate of interest on the indexed bonds will be lower than identical maturity 'true' dollar bonds reflecting the lower real rate of interest in the controlled domestic market. The differential between the interest yield on pseudo and true dollar bonds is one indication of the degree of severity of capital flow restrictions.

But it is conceivable that dollar indexation could become so popular that dollar notes could partially replace domestic money as the medium of exchange. That could occur in two ways.

First top credit status corporations could issue dollar indexed notes in bearer form in denominations of say $100 upwards. Banks themselves would be best placed probably to undertake such an operation. They would match dollar-indexed liabilities with dollar-indexed assets. They would find many borrowers willing to borrow on a dollar-indexed basis since the potential volatility of the liability in real terms would be less than for lira denomination.

Second the government itself might issue bearer dollar-indexed notes. If they came to be acceptable as medium of exchange, their yield would drop possibly to zero reflecting a growing convenience return to their holders. The government could increase the popularity of its dollar notes as the medium of exchange by accepting them in payment for its own bills – for example taxation.

The monetisation of dollar-indexed paper would occur only in highly unstable conditions and should not be regarded as more than curiosity. The issue of dollar-indexed bonds is of more general interest and could well be included in stabilisation packages of governments slowing inflation rates down from 20 per cent + to single digits.

When inflation reaches double digits the domestic bond market usually becomes sick. Experience of the 1970s shows that sustained inflation at that rate brings to a halt long-term bond issues by private sector corporations. The government can raise bond finance only at extremely high rates so as to provide a premium to investors in compensation for volatility of real returns. If the government switches instead to issuing dollar-indexed paper, it must pay a much smaller effective risk premium and hunger for the paper will be great. The temptation to use the printing press as alternative to the issue of bonds is reduced.

A stabilisation package's ingredients include normally a phasing down of the rate of monetary growth and the replacement of revenue from inflation tax with other taxes. Fiscal rearrangements take time whilst the reduction of inflation follows immediately on the slowdown of monetary growth. The issue of dollar-indexed paper provides a way of meeting the shortfall in a context where issue of local currency debt or official borrowing abroad would be exorbitantly expensive.

The technique of monetary stabilisation by the introduction of foreign currency indexed debt has been used in a variety of circumstances. The most dramatic was the innovation of the rentenmark and valorised bonds in the latter days of the great German hyperinflation of 1923.

INDEXATION TO THE GENERAL PRICE LEVEL

The issue of dollar-indexed debt has been more common historically than of general price-indexed debt. One explanation is that in extreme inflationary circumstances general price indices are often distorted or very inexact. Borrowers and lenders prefer then to use as the unit of account a price quoted in the market – the exchange rate – rather than an artificially constructed index. Further over long periods of time movement of a general price index is difficult to interpret. The qualities of component goods in the index change due to technological progress. General price level indexation is therefore most suitable for short to medium maturity instruments.

Indexed bonds could take many forms. If the real interest rate is negative, careful construction is needed. Suppose the real interest yield that five-year indexed bonds could sell at is —2 per cent per annum. The corporation or government would issue notes with face value of say L1000 (lire are the assumed local currency). The face value would be indexed to the general price level. The notes would be issued at a price of L1100. The real loss after five years would be L100 in base year lire, equivalent to an annual real loss at the rate of —2 per cent.

To provide evidence of its creditworthiness the corporation could set up a sinking fund which would re-purchase in the market say 5 per cent of outstanding stock each year. That would serve a similar function to coupon payments on normal bonds – a prepayment in real terms of a portion of outstanding debt.

Prices of indexed bonds would be more volatile in small open economies than in large ones. In Chapter 1 (p. 13) the greater volatility was discussed of interest rates on small than on large currencies. That was due to their greater exposure to foreign exchange market influences. Indexed notes denominated in small currencies would be exposed similarly as real interest rates tended to reflect expected real exchange rate movements.

Real interest rates, and hence the price of indexed notes, are potentially more volatile in countries which restrict the free flow of capital internationally. The domestic rate of return can fluctuate below that obtainable in the capital markets of countries with freely tradable currencies. The expected real interest rate on five-year dollar bonds has been substantially less volatile than on pound or lira bonds during the past decade.

The failure of indexed notes to be issued in high inflation-prone countries must be attributed largely to fiscal structures. According to tax codes nominal profits are taxable. The difference between purchase price of the note and maturity value – in nominal terms – would be taxed. If instead escalation payments received by the investor were tax free and were tax-deductible for the borrower, indexed notes would presumably be popular. The real cost of borrowing would be reduced as no premium would be paid to lenders in compensation for inflation risk. The indexed form eliminates fluctuations of real return due to an uncertain inflation rate.

The changed treatment for tax purposes of indexed debt would be the catalyst to almost complete indexation of the fiscal structure.

Corporations would buy back rapidly outstanding nominal debt and issue indexed debt instead, its real cost being less. Debt instruments would have their attractiveness increased relative to equities. The tax authorities would have to index promptly capital gains taxation, if resulting leverage ratios of corporate capital structures were thought undesirable. Capital gains tax bears most heavily on the equity holder.

The issue of indexed notes simplifies the administrative task of indexing income tax. Inflation deductions are categorised in the form of debt instruments. Accountants and tax officials do not need to estimate and check allowances themselves.

FREE LUNCH FALLACIES

The history of official stabilisation in commodity markets extends back to biblical times. Pharaoh had a dream in which seven lean cows followed seven fat cows. The lean cows ate up the fat ones. Pharaoh's courtiers could not provide explanations of the dream. Joseph was summoned. He interpreted the dream as foreboding seven years of plentiful harvest followed by seven years of famine. In consequence warehouses were built and surplus was stored during the seven years of plenty. In the subsequent famine the people of Egypt were saved from starvation.

Today there is no shortage of courtiers who lay claim to dreams of future famine. They rarely act on divine insight and speculate on uncertain predictions about the future as do private speculators. Some pretend to be able to operate stabilisation schemes at zero cost. On closer examination all such plans are built on 'free lunch' fallacies.

FORWARD INTERVENTION IN CURRENCY MARKETS

It is sometimes argued that official intervention in the forward market is less costly than spot market intervention in the use of foreign exchange reserves. The subject of forward intervention is complex and is discussed further in Chapter 4. The purpose here is limited to unravelling the free lunch fallacy in the proposition.

In the years 1964–7 the Bank of England intervened persistently in the forward sterling market. The technique involved purchasing forward sterling from UK banks. By so narrowing the forward discount on sterling against the dollar, it became profitable to switch from dollars into domestic pounds on a covered basis. It was possible to earn more by selling dollars spot for pounds, investing in London pound CDs and selling pounds forward for dollars than from investing in identical maturity euro-dollar deposits. The forward exchange operation thus induced spot purchases of pounds without direct dollar borrowing or use of foreign exchange reserves by the British Government.

The Bank of England was effectively gaining a free lunch at the expense of the shareholders in British banks with which it arranged the forward deals. The bank had a large forward commitment to the Bank of England having sold pounds forward for dollars. The underlying credit risk was whether the Bank could ultimately find the dollars to honour its contracts. In the international capital markets banks would have demanded a premium to bear that risk. No premium was paid to UK banks: they did not bargain with the Bank of England fearing that they might incur its disfavour which would have costly consequences for their domestic operations.

Yet the risk that UK banks undertook in selling pounds forward to the Bank of England must have curtailed their investment in other risk ventures which would have been more profitable. Indirectly a subsidy was paid to the British monetary authorities by bank shareholders. They paid for the free lunch.

FORWARD INTERVENTION IN METAL MARKETS

Grandiose plans for buffer stocks flounder normally on problems of finance. Sometimes forward intervention has been proposed as an alternative. Official stabilisation would be operated by buying or selling metal forward. By pushing up the forward price arbitragers are induced to purchase the metal spot and sell it forward. They earn more than the going interest rate. It appears therefore that the financing load is borne by private arbitragers. The flaw is that there must be some credit guarantee behind the contracts into which the buffer stock enters.

Speculators and arbitragers have no reason to provide a free lunch for the buffer stock in the metal markets. Any effect on the spot price that forward intervention has could be effected at no greater cost in the spot market. If the buffer stock can provide credit guarantees in the forward market, it is also able to raise finance to operate in the spot too.

The scope of operation of buffer stocks in commodities is less than in currencies. The buffer stock manager should cease buying a commodity when the expected capital gain is less than the financing and storage costs. Indeed he should dispose of inventory to traders deriving convenience yield from owning the commodity.

Once the buffer stock has been run down to zero the manager's operations are halted. He cannot issue commodity paper to sell in the spot market that would be a perfect substitute for the physical commodity. He is less fortunate in that respect than his central bank counterpart in the currency market.

Skyrocketing prices based on natural shortages are a feature peculiar to commodity markets. Coffee crop failures in Brazil and drought in the Prairies are events that make and disperse fortunes. The speculative climate of the currency world is more temperate.

4 Too Few Speculators?

'Who are you?' said the Caterpillar. 'I – I hardly know, sir, just at present – at least I know who I was when I got up this morning, but I think I must have changed several times since then'.
'I don't see' said the Caterpillar.
'I'm afraid I can't put it more clearly' Alice replied very politely 'for I can't understand it myself to begin with: and being so many different sizes in a day is very distressing'.
'It isn't' said the Caterpillar.

Alice in Wonderland

The closing of the US 'gold window' in August 1971 marked neither the end of the fixed exchange rate world nor the dawn of freely floating currencies. Rather conformity in international exchange rate practices ceased to be a generally acceptable goal. Each central bank now chooses its own exchange regime – freely floating, adjustable peg, controlled floating or fixed. Each system is promoted by salesmen who resort sometimes to simplification and exaggeration. 'The conclusion is that good advice, whomever it comes from, depends on the shrewdness of the prince who seeks it' (Machiavelli).

Some of the most ardent supporters of freely floating exchange rates have used an accounting trick to sell their system. The device has been unfortunate as it has diverted attention from the fundamental problem of how to maximise the efficient working of a free currency market.

THREE TYPES OF SPECULATOR

There are three basic types of operator in the foreign exchange markets and they may be combined in the same person. The *investor* buys a currency either to purchase assets in the country of issue or as a long-run component of his portfolio. Many for example buy Swiss francs, US dollars, and West German marks, along with gold, with the intention of holding them until 'Kingdom come' The *trader* buys a currency to settle invoices for goods and services. The *speculator* operates by spotting when interest rate differentials between currencies are more or less than expected exchange rate movements.

The debate between supporters of the differing currency systems is based mainly on differing views of the efficiency of the speculative function. In an adjustable peg system a high proportion of speculation is conducted by the central bank and is equal to the official settlements balance of payments surplus or deficit.

In a free float all speculation is by private operators and the balance of payments deficit on an official settlements basis is identically zero. The claim follows that the balance of payments balances automatically if the currency floats freely. That is simply a statement of an accounting identity. In economic reality, the speculative function of absorbing excess supplies of currencies from investors and traders – or conversely – has been wholly relinquished by governmental authorities.

If speculators (private or public) were absent from the currency markets, fluctuations in exchange rates would be great. The proposition can be illustrated for a country which has a shortfall of exports due to an exceptionally cold winter. The exchange rate would have to plummet to a level that would reduce demand for imports by an equal amount during the period of shortfall. An abrupt change in consumption patterns would be enforced.

The outcome would have been different if positions were assumed by currency speculators. They would have mopped up the excess supplies of currency corresponding to the temporary export short-fall thereby permitting the country to run a trade deficit. The exchange rate fall would have been much less and there would have been hardly any immediate cutback in consumption. The currency depreciation needs now to be sufficient only to generate a trade surplus equal to the temporary deficit over a longer period of time. As the surplus begins to be realized speculators dispose gradually of their currency inventories.

Proponents of controlled floating would argue that speculators tend to be misinformed, risk averse and their horizons short. Consider the above example of an export shortfall. The exchange rate might have to fall far below what is necessary to generate a trade surplus over the longer run before a sufficient number of speculators are tempted to assume the risk of mopping up excess currency supplies.

Free floaters would respond that private speculators are longer-sighted than politicians for whom one week may be a long time. Further they have a profit incentive to use available information correctly.

It is difficult to design a form of government speculation in the currency market that is complimentary to private speculation. Official intervention itself introduces usually a new hazard. Private speculators must guess the intervention tactics of the public speculator.

In order to consider further the debate between the advocates of free and controlled floating the nature of the speculative function must be studied. The problem of combining private and public speculation is returned to in Chapter 6.

FIRST-, SECOND-AND THIRD-ORDER SPECULATION

First-order speculators react to currency shortage or glut in the present. Speculative reaction to the export short-fall due to adverse weather conditions was one example. Others would include reaction to a temporary currency demand due to the bunching of some large export receipts; speculators would then short-sell. In the absence of first-order speculation in a given period, the exchange rate would move abruptly in response to such current shocks.

Second-order speculators react to currency shortage or glut expected in future periods possibly months or years ahead. Their intervention in the spot market serves to smooth out abrupt exchange rate changes anticipated in the future rather than the present. A country may have large prospective oil revenues growing exponentially from about two years into the future. Second-order speculators would build up their currency inventories now in anticipation of large trade surpluses in the future when a currency shortage would be expected. The speculative purchases cause the exchange rate to appreciate sooner and so induce larger trade deficits before the oil flows. Second-order speculation should smooth consumption over time. Second- is more hazardous than first-order speculation because its subject is an uncertain future rather than a certain present discontinuity in an international trade or capital flow.

Third-order speculators neither absorb excess supplies nor short-sell currency in demand. Their operations are directed at spotting discrepancies in the relation of futures prices to each other. For example the speculator may believe that three-month deutsch-marks are too cheap relative to six-month deutschmarks (both in terms of US dollars) and that the relationship will correct itself during the next three-month period. He would then buy three-month deutschmarks and simultaneously sell six-month deutsch-marks intending to close his positions when the correct relation is realized. If all euro-rates are at covered parity with each other, his operation is equivalent to borrowing three-month euro-dollars, lending six-month euro-dollars; borrwoing six-month euro-deutschmarks and lending three-month euro-deutschmarks.

The effect of the third-order speculator's action is to widen the differential between three-month euro-dollars and euro-deutschmarks and narrow it for six-month maturities. No flows are induced across the exchanges in contrast to the effect of first- and second-order speculation. Rather a smoothing of interest rate differentials over time is accomplished.

SPECULATION IN RESTRICTED CURRENCY REGIMES

First- and second-order speculation is limited in scope in restricted currencies. Short-selling the currency in the spot market is normally difficult and buying it to hold in domestic form is not attractive because interest rates are non-competitive internationally. In practice restrictions tend to bear more heavily on short-selling. Restricted currencies experience therefore periods of artificial strength similar to the phenomenon of commodity booms discussed at the end of Chapter 3. As with commodities restricted currencies can be sold freely in future markets (at least by non-residents) but it is not easy to borrow either one in 'physical' form to sell spot.

The analogy between commodity and restricted currency invest-ment can be extended further. During a recessionary period some base metals may become investment commodities. Excess in-ventories are so large that convenience rent falls to zero and pure investors can justify holding the commodity in physical form. The ratio of forward to spot price then approximates storage and financing costs.

Restricted currencies are not suitable candidates normally in domestic form for the international investor to hold (see Chapter 1, p. 21). During periods of currency glut they may undergo a transformation. The interest rate in the domestic money market rises to a level which is competitive internationally.

The convenience rent of a restricted currency is measured by the differential between its euro- and domestic market interest rate. Under conditions of currency glut – deriving from a large trade deficit or capital flight – the differential and hence the convenience rent falls to zero. Speculators then mop up the currency as they would a freely tradable one. So long as the convenience rent remained positive the only speculators who purchased spot currency would be those who derived some convenience yield from holding it domestically. Other speculators would have purchased the currency only in a forward form (including its euro-version). Such forward operations would play no direct part in the absorption of excess currency.

During a period of currency shortage speculators will freely short-sell it in the forward but not in the spot market. Short sales are restricted there. Non-residents are generally not permitted to borrow restricted currencies from domestic banks. The forward discount on the currency will so widen considerably and the euro-rate can reach sometimes astronomical levels. Domestic interest rates and the spot exchange rate are insulated to a considerable extent and so the convenience rent on domestic deposits increases sharply. Unlike in the case of currency glut there is no tendency in extreme conditions for the qualities of freely tradable currencies to be assumed. Further if the maximum maturity of forward contracts is for less than the expected period of shortage, even the reaction of convenience rent will not occur.

The history of sterling illustrates well the properties of restricted currency exchange rate behaviour. During much of 1974–6 sterling was considerably overvalued relative to the inflation performance of the UK. The divergence was caused by a build-up of OPEC reserves in domestic sterling. Many exchange market participants realised at the time that the strength of the pound was a temporary phenomenon. Profitable speculation based on that belief was difficult. Bears could sell pounds short in the forward market, but for maturities beyond one year such transactions are difficult to accomplish. Sterling's strength could easily have persisted for a year under continuing OPEC investment pressure. If the pound had been freely tradable, many speculators would have borrowed pounds for periods of more than one year to finance non-pound denominated operations. They would have thus effectively short-sold pounds in the spot market and have caused the spot rate to fall earlier. In the event UK restrictions denied them the opportunity.

The fundamental over-valuation of the pound in 1974 was apparent from the behaviour of convenience rent on domestic pounds. The euro-pound, domestic-pound interest rate differential was persistently high reflecting speculative selling pressure on forward sterling quotes. That the Arab nations continued to pile up domestic rather than euro-pound deposits must be attributed mainly to a lack of financial sophistication and a desire to diversify political risks.

When the pound's first crash occured in Spring 1976 the convenience rent on domestic pound deposits was eliminated quickly. The differential between interest rates on domestic and euro-pounds disappeared. That signified that speculators were now purchasing pounds spot to hold in domestic form. They believed the pound to have fallen to a low enough level for domestic deposits to offer an internationally competitive rate of return given prospective future demand conditions in the sterling exchange market.

By the summer of 1976 the euro-domestic pound differential had again widened as there developed a crisis of confidence in the capability of the UK government to control its expenditure. A further exchange rate fall and the raising of large dollar loans enticed speculators to purchase sufficient spot pounds to prevent the rate falling below its then level of $1·77. Convenience rent on domestic pounds was again eliminated and UK pound deposits became temporarily 'eligible' for inclusion in the portfolio of international investors. A further cycle in convenience rent occurred before 1976 was out.

By the beginning of 1977 sterling had returned to a phase of being subject to net demand by investors and traders. The current account in the UK's balance of payments swung towards balance. New exchange restrictions on lending pounds to finance international trade were responsible for net demand for pounds of as much as $1·5 billion within six months. The UK authorities suspected that a substantial part of the demand for pounds was transitory and entered the market themselves as huge short-sellers of spot pounds. They had doubled their foreign exchange reserves by end-June 1977.

Many economic commentators criticised the UK government for not permitting the pound exchange rate to float freely in 1977. They hoped that an appreciating pound would reduce domestic inflationary pressures. The criticism was in part misplaced. Only in a free float accompanied by continuing restricted tradability is it certain that the pound would have floated up. If short-selling had been freely permitted, speculators would have resisted upward movement of the rate realising the temporary nature of some of the net demand for pounds. Because its own rules prevented such stabilising speculation, the Bank of England assumed that function.

Unlike in the 1974–5 period of heavy OPEC demand for pounds the convenience rent on domestic pounds was zero for most of the first half of 1977. The difference can be explained by the heavy official short-selling of pounds that characterised 1977. Private speculators became typically purchasers of forward pounds. They believed the discount of the forward pound below its officially depressed spot level to exaggerate expected depreciation. The forward discount narrowed only slowly due to the official policy of maintaining high domestic interest rates. Covered arbitrage flows with euro-dollars led therefore to downward pressure on the forward pound.

The analysis of the pound's predisposition towards periods of artificial strength could be repeated in almost identical form for the French franc, Italian lira, Spanish peseta, Mexican peso or Scandinavian currencies. All are difficult to short-sell in the spot market and their domestic form becomes unattractive to the international investor when they are scarce.

Throughout the first six months of 1977 the Spanish central bank purchased on a massive scale pesetas in the foreign exchange market. The purpose was to defend the official dollar parity. Speculators knew that the official purchases of pesetas could not continue for long and they sold pesetas forward. The forward discount on pesetas against dollars was sometimes as high as 4 per cent per month. Domestic Spanish interest rates never exceeded $1\frac{1}{2}$ per cent per month. The resulting 30 per cent per annum convenience rent on domestic pesetas was a measure of their extreme artificial shortage. The peseta shortage was not natural, as with commodities in famine, but a product of Spanish exchange restrictions.

SPECULATION IN SMALL CURRENCIES

Low-cost market-making is essential to the success of a free float. If bid-offer spreads in the currency market are wide, significant exchange rate movements can occur without profitable stabilising speculation being possible. The currency's high transaction costs would decrease further its attractiveness.

Market-makers in a small currency's exchange market experience low turnover relative to inventory. Bid-offer spreads tend therefore to be wide. A central bank has two possible methods of promoting lower spreads.

The central bank could encourage trading in the currency to be concentrated in limited time periods each day. It would become customary for currency traders to meet daily at say midday on the Bourse to transact business. Operators would instruct their brokers to effect their orders only on the floor of the Bourse to benefit from the lower transaction costs there. The time compression of foreign exchange business increases the ratio of turnover to inventory for market-makers and reduces bid-offer spreads. The compression device is used in many European currency centres including Brussels, Amsterdam and Vienna and also in the London gold and silver bullion markets and the London Metal Exchange. The 'fixing' price is announced at lunch-time each day.

Alternatively the central bank of a small currency may choose to assume the role of market-maker itself, and yet not influence the price of foreign exchange. To promote use of its currency, say dinars, the central bank quotes a narrower bid-offer spread than would be profitable for any private market-maker. Other banks and dealers come to act as the central bank's agent in the foreign exchange market. They intend to re-sell immediately dinars offered them and re-buy dinars for which they are bid by transacting with the central bank. All foreign exchange business involving the dinar is so conducted ultimately with the only market-maker. If the dinar is still to float freely, the central bank must quote an exchange rate that is consistent with zero net accumulation of foreign exchange reserves. The official market-maker (central bank) should not assume speculative positions on its own behalf. Private speculators, like most other transactors in the currency, deal with agents of the central bank.

The central bank may decide against assuming for itself the role of sole market-maker. It may then prefer to peg the exchange rate to a larger denominator and share market-making with banks. The bond within which the exchange rate was pegged would have to be narrow if the bid-offer spreads quoted by market-makers are to be significantly narrower than in a free float. The central bank would have to intervene frequently to prevent the exchange rate breaking through its limits.

Dealers in a pegged currency act often as agents of the central bank rather than as independent market-makers. Private market-making so evaporates whenever the floor or ceiling of the intervention band is reached and the central bank operates to prevent a breach.

Consider a hypothetical crisis in the European Snake. The Belgian franc has fallen to its floor of 15·60 francs/DM. The National Bank of Belgium stands ready to sell deutschmarks for each 15·60 francs offered. Banks dealing in francs then quote bid and offer rates for deutschmarks equal to 15·60 francs/deutschmarks minus and plus brokerage commission respectively. Thus the bank would quote 15·50–15·70 DM if commission was 0·10 francs/DM. The franc dealer would tend to accumulate excess franc inventories because the National Bank's intervention causes deutschmarks to be cheap relative to their free market equilibrium price. The dealer off-loads his franc inventories at the National Bank who pays him 15·60 francs/DM.

The bid-offer spread quoted by the franc dealer is not evidence of independent market-making but of built-in commission. When an exchange rate knocks against an intervention limit its bid-offer spread in the spot market narrows typically. The narrowing is symptomatic of market-makers being metamorphosed into central bank agents.

SPECULATION IN TWO-TIERED CURRENCY MARKETS

Two-tiered markets involve the channelling of all financial-type-transactions through a separate market from commercial (see Chapter 1, p. 29). First- and second-order speculation are in theory impossible in the commercial tier because international borrowing and lending transactions must be effected through the financial exchange market. Stabilisation of the commercial exchange rate is the exclusive function of the government and its agencies. Often the rate is pegged to another currency. Third-order speculation can occur in the commercial tier. It takes the form of buying or selling the commercial currency for forward delivery. Speculators in aggregate move the forward price towards their expected future spot price. If their estimate is efficient, the basis of commercial decision-taking is improved. Businessmen use forward prices as an input to future production and buying policy decisions.

First- and second-order speculative operations are possible in the financial tier of the foreign exchange market. Although net international capital flows are zero – assuming zero official intervention in the financial market – speculation can determine their composition over time. Suppose a large purchase of Belgian francs financiers is made by a US corporation buying a subsidiary in Belgium. Speculators would borrow francs from a Brussels bank and sell them spot in the financier market for dollars to meet the temporary shortage. They would hope to reverse the transaction at a future date when the franc financier will have depreciated by more than the interest rate differential between francs financiers and dollars.

The speculators' operations prevent the financier exchange rate from rising as sharply as would be required to induce enough Belgian investment demand for dollars equal to the amount being sold by the US corporation. Investment demand is more sluggish than speculative demand in the short-run. Time is needed to appraise potential portfolio and direct investments. By absorbing excess dollars in the short-run the speculator enables them to be 'carried over' until longer term placements have been considered. In the short-run the inflow of dollars to Belgium from the US corporation is matched by a speculative outflow of francs financiers into dollars. In the longer term the speculative outflows return to finance an outflow of portfolio or direct investment.

WHO IS THE CURRENCY SPECULATOR?

The role of the currency speculator has been described. But who is the speculator? Not many of us know people who claim to live by speculative expertise in the currency market. Speculation is a high risk activity and speculators tend to have standby occupations. A businessman trading on the Chicago IMM or an oil sheik taking a currency position with a Zurich bank both fulfil speculative functions. Speculation is not the sole occupation of either.

The speculator must be an individualist. At a time of currency glut he must mop up the surplus: during times of currency famine he must again take a longer-term view and short-sell.

Individualism is not enough. The speculator must also be well endowed with funds. Transaction costs on small deals are high and small speculators would not find it profitable to smooth out fluctuations that were not significantly greater. In practice the small speculator confines his operations to taking long-run views on a currency based on predicted changes in fundamental factors. They include money supply and balance of payments developments. Their exact timing is difficult and the speculator often does not expect to close his position profitably until several months have passed and a sizable percentage profit has been made. Transaction costs relative to profit should decrease with the length of time over which the position is taken.

Short-run speculation, often on a day-to-day basis, is normally profitable only for those dealing in millions of dollars. In practice this category of speculator includes governments, central banks, commercial banks and multi-national corporations. Dealers in these institutions are authorised often to take short-term speculative positions, while longer-term strategic ones would be frowned upon. A brave foreign exchange dealer who believes that the US dollar would rise on an expected improved US trade performance would not receive much sympathy if, after one week, a significant loss was recorded on his long position. Large institutions prefer a safe life. They are not the climbers of the Mount Everests in the currency market.

BANKS AS SPECULATORS

Banks are best placed to speculate on very small exchange rate fluctuations, primarily on a day-to-day basis. They can deal in large volumes and are often themselves market-makers in the currency markets. Their transaction costs are hence minimal.

Banks specialise in smoothing fluctuations due to 'technical' factors. Their dealers are trained to spot exchange rate movements due to profit-taking, bunched conversions into local currency from foreign bond issues or news items that are digested slowly by the market. The bank dealer must be reasonably confident that his expected exchange rate movement will occur within twenty-four hours and certainly not much longer than one week. His counterpart in the commodity markets is the 'scalper' who hopes to profit from fluctuations that will be smoothed out within one day. The scalper buys for example when he believes the price to have been temporarily depressed by a large selling-order.

Banks tend to shy away from taking longer-term views on currencies and from assuming strategic open positions. The business of currency speculation is risky and is not considered generally a suitable activity for banks. Their extremely high ratio of debt (including deposits) to equity liabilities, and the high proportion of short-term debt, make risky investment inappropriate. The American banks are the most conservative about assuming speculative positions in currencies. Some German and Swiss banks are inclined to regard foreign exchange speculation as a continuing business activity.

Bank conservatism is enforced sometimes by statute. Following the Herstatt bank failure of 1974 the German authorities restricted speculation by resident banks. At the end of each business day banks should not have an open position (spot and forward combined) of more than 30 per cent of their own funds (capital plus reserves). Similar rules exist in many states. They can often be avoided by banks booking their speculative transactions through offshore subsidiaries.

SPECULATION ROUND THE CLOCK

Exchange rate movements in a financial centre are equally likely to rise as fall during the business day. Discontinuous exchange rate shift, with a bias of direction, should be expected between today's closing and tomorrow's opening rate. These propositions about currency motion follow from the procedure for calculating interest due on deposits and loans.

Interest is calculated on balances outstanding at the close of business each day. If a dealer carries an open currency position overnight, he must expect an exchange rate movement at least equal to the additional interest cost. Interest charges are not a consideration in intra-day trading where speculative positions are justified so long as an exchange rate fluctuation greater than transaction costs is expected.

If speculation is competitive, speculators should not all expect an exchange rate trend in the same direction during trading hours. That would imply a non-exploited speculative profit from selling the currency at opening time and re-buying it before the close. Competitive speculators can in aggregate anticipate a sequence of downward shifts each night equal to the cost of running short positions overnight.

Short-sellers of a weak currency close their positions before the end of the business day, if they do not expect a price decline overnight equal to interest cost. Some of these same speculators will re-open their short position the following morning intending at first to take an intra-day view. The pattern of closing short positions and re-opening next morning reinforces the tendency of exchange rates to jump overnight. The pattern is particularly noticeable at week-ends when three days' interest cost would become due.

Foreign exchange trading occurs now in many different time zones. Gap periods exist however when all markets are simultaneously closed. If these gaps were plugged by the emergence of extended trading periods, would the pattern of discontinuous exchange rate movements overnight be eliminated? Could the short-seller, by closing his position in one centre as business finishes and immediately re-opening it in a centre still trading, avoid overnight interest costs?

There is a flaw in the seeming perpetual motion machine that allows the passing of time without the incurring of interest charges. Each time a position is closed and re-opened a bid-offer spread is paid. Cumulative bid-offer spread charged on the twenty-four circuit of financial centres would be in excess of overnight interest cost in one centre.

MULTINATIONAL SPECULATORS

Multinationals are faced continuously with currency decisions. Should assets in France be hedged against a franc depreciation? Should deutschmarks be bought forward to pay invoices due in one month? Should finance for an oil project in the North Sea be raised in deutschmarks or dollars?

Multinationals are more predisposed to assuming speculative positions than banks. Their ordinary business activities are often riskier than those of banks: the risk of foreign exchange speculation is more acceptable for them. The multinational's capital structure is less levered and longer-term compared to a bank's. They are therefore less circumscribed structurally from speculating.

In contrast to banks multinationals follow rarely a policy of hedging all foreign exchange risk exposure by the close of business each day. The multinational treasurer does not have to justify daily to his colleagues each and every speculative position that has been assumed. Profit and loss on unhedged assets and liabilities is not calculated daily as for the bank dealer. There is scope for the multinational treasurer to 'fudge' foreign exchange speculation profits and losses into more general accounts. Banks in contrast must call foreign exchange spades a spade. Speculative positions are – if bank internal rules are effective – visible to all concerned.

The multinational treasurer is inclined to take short-to medium-term strategic views on currency movements. He is not a market-maker in foreign exchange and it would be too expensive to trade intra-day on technical factors. He will of course assess technical factors when choosing the cheapest time to effect an exchange transaction within a limited period. If the treasurer has a large deutschmark purchase to make within twenty-four hours, he will study all possible influences on the intra-day deutschmark exchange rate fluctuations.

The multinational treasurer must sometimes take long-term currency decisions, even if by default. Suppose the corporation makes a direct investment in France. Access of non-residents to the French bond market is forbidden. The treasurer must choose between long-term finance in other currency bond markets. His choice would be limited since most countries control the issue of debt by non-residents in their bond market. His selection would most likely be between Canadian dollars, US dollars, West German marks and Swiss francs.

The treasurer who bases his bond decision on a positive long-term currency view is a rarity. Most, in the French problem described, would raise dollar finance because dollar bond markets are the broadest. Some treasurers adopt a policy of diversifying over time the denomination of their borrowing between the three dream currencies – US dollars, West German marks and Swiss francs.

The exceptional treasurer might decide to issue five-year notes in deutschmarks rather than dollars because he believes that West German trade account will plunge into deficit within two years. There would be then a glut of deutschmarks and their exchange rate would fall. The treasurer believes further that the interest rate differential between five-year deutschmark and dollar notes discounts adequately that development.

Five years is a long time in the life of a corporate treasurer. He wants quick rewards. Long-term speculative positions are taken mainly by individuals. Their scene of action is the euro-bond market.

SPECULATION FROM SWITZERLAND

Various guesses have been hazarded on the amount of non-resident funds (including securities) in the safe-keeping of Swiss banks. None are less than $100 billion. Many obstacles prevent active management of these funds by their ultimate owners. Therefore investments are made with a longer anticipated holding period. On the infrequent occasions that the client can review actively his portfolio he must choose between accentuating different currencies. He knows that many months or years may pass before his currency decision can be reversed.

Not all clients make a positive choice of currency based on a calculation of long term exchange rate movements. They may simply adopt standard proportions for each currency's representation in their portfolios, say US $50 per cent, Sw. fr. 25 per cent, DM 25 per cent. Selection of those proportions is symptomatic of a client who dreams in three currency colours with a heavy dollar emphasis.

Some clients attempt to increase their portfolio returns by choosing astutely currency denomination of their assets. They analyse carefully whether to place new liquid funds in euro-dollar, deutschmark, guilder, Swiss franc or Canadian dollar bonds.

Funds find their way to Switzerland to escape rapacious tax collectors and the confines of soft money investment. Owners are unlikely to reinvest their 'freed' funds in Italian lira or Spanish peseta bonds. They favour euro-bonds which are typically in hard currency, always in bearer form and not subject to withholding tax. Currencies whose bonds do not exist in euro-form and which are eschewed by Swiss account investors are deprived of the benefits of longer-term speculative interest.

In the world of currencies nothing succeeds like hardness and nothing fails like softness. A hard currency, popular with investors, enjoy fully the benefits of speculation. A soft currency, unpopular and with restricted tradability, may react with alarming volatility to changing economic fundamentals. Lack of short-sellers causes the currency to suffer from periods of artificial strength. Lack of international investors in bonds of soft currency denomination eclipse longer term considerations which cannot in consequence influence the exchange market. The soft money exchange rate is thus particularly sensitive to short-run economic developments.

Swiss account investors can affect exchange rates in both directions by their long-term speculative decisions. Suppose astute Swiss clients display a tendency to switch from euro-deutschmark to euro-dollar bonds believing that the deutschmark is fundamentally weak over the longer-term. Euro-deutschmark bond yields react upwards and increase relative to domestic German bonds. So Germans are induced to switch from domestic bonds into the now higher yielding euro-deutschmark bonds. They sell deutschmarks for dollars to purchase the euro-deutschmark bonds from the Swiss investor who uses the dollars to purchase euro-dollar bonds.

The sellers of euro-deutschmark bonds are in effect first-order speculators in the deutschmark exchange market. Their time horizons are abnormally long. They set up a chain of transactions which culminate in a spot sale of deutschmarks for dollars. The resulting downward drift of the deutschmark anticipates feared far-off developments in the German economy.

SPECULATIVE PROFITS

Long-term currency speculation using bond instruments is potentially the most profitable. Long-term interest rates are influenced less than short-term by exchange rate expectations and more by domestic inflation considerations. The differential between long-term interest rates on currencies is therefore often substantially different from the expected exchange rate movement.

Bond investment is most attractive as a vehicle of currency speculation to those placing liquid funds. The high transaction costs of switching between bonds deter currency speculation from assuming that form. Competition is so reduced in the international bond markets for currency speculators well-endowed with cash. They avoid the cost of first selling bonds to realize cash for new acquisitions.

Competition between currency speculators is most intense in the international money markets where the transaction costs are lowest. There the distinction between speculating by switching and by placing fresh funds is least important. The average bid-offer spread on a euro-bond is $\frac{1}{2}$ per cent, compared to $\frac{1}{8}$ per cent on a three-month certificate of deposit. The small investor, dealing in amounts of \$10,000, pays often 'round-trip' commissions of a further $\frac{3}{4}$ per cent on euro-bond transactions. Exchange rate expectations must change by more than transaction costs to justify the speculative operation of switching between bonds of different currency denomination. Indeed to tempt a speculator to incur certain transaction cost outlays now, his expected gain – which is very uncertain – should be much greater.

Currency speculation in the euro-bond markets is particularly suitable for those investors who are of constant mind and therefore unlikely to switch between bonds. Their potential profit is greater than that of the currency speculator in the international money market. There competition is keener between speculators because a higher proportion of transactions are motivated by exchange rate expectations.

INTEREST RATE AND CURRENCY SPECULATION DISTINGUISHED

If a currency speculator deals in instruments whose maturities are different from his trading horizon, he is also implicitly speculating on interest rate movements. Suppose he borrows dollars and buys a three-month euro-deutschmark deposit yet intends to close his position after not more than one month. At that time the exchange rate may have moved as expected, but an unexpected deutschmark interest rate rise may have occurred. His gain will then be less than anticipated because he will incur extra interest cost in borrowing two-month deutschmarks to close his deutschmark position.

Bank currency dealers try to separate currency and interest rate speculation into separate transactions. Their trading horizon is often not much more than one day. Profit and loss is assessed daily and they do not sit on positions for long. If a dealer believes that the deutschmark will appreciate overnight, he buys deutschmark for delivery tomorrow. Suppose he also believes that the three-month interest rate on euro-deutschmarks will soon rise relative to that on euro-dollars. He would then borrow euro-deutschmarks for one week and lend them for three months. He would simultaneously borrow dollars for three months and lend them for one week. He would hope to reverse all transactions to show a net profit before the end of one week.

Separation of interest and exchange rate speculation is particularly important when trading restricted currencies. Limits on arbitrage between the domestic, euro- and forward markets lead to greater volatility of forward currency quotations. Forward rates are not tied to domestic interest rates by covered arbitrage flows and are therefore more exposed to exchange rate expectations. Exchange restrictions cut the forward currency quotes off from the pull of gravity of the domestic credit market.

The Swedish kroner is an example of a restricted currency. Between the end of June and the beginning of September 1977 the one-month forward discount on kroners against the US dollar widened from 8 per cent to 40 per cent, and narrowed back to 8 per cent (all discounts expressed at annual rates). In June the foreign exchange market believed already that a kroner devaluation was imminent. The Swedish central bank continued to support the kroner at its official parity within the European Snake until the end of August. Then the kroner was devalued by 10 per cent.

There is no euro-market in Swedish kroners. A foreign exchange dealer is limited effectively to two methods of speculating as a bear on kroners. He can sell them spot (to deliver in two days' time), engage in forward-forward transactions or both. If he believes that the rate will be devalued within two days, he sells kroners spot hoping to buy them at a cheaper rate on delivery day. Suppose he anticipates a more distant devaluation, but believes that within a week the three-month forward discount will have widened from 20 to 30 per cent (at annual rates). That belief would be based on a prediction that exchange market sentiment towards the kroner would become even more pessimistic. The dealer then buys kroners one week forward and sells them three months forward for dollars. The operation is termed a 'forward-forward' transaction. The dealer hopes to close profitably his positions within a week.

ROYAL FLUSH

The potential profits from forward-forward speculation tend to be greater in restricted than freely tradable currencies. The forward exchange rate of a restricted currency is volatile due to its insulation from the stabilising influence of covered interest arbitrage flows. The rewards from separating speculation on the daily movements of the spot exchange rate from forward-forward speculation are consequently greater.

Suppose the kroner dealer had lacked the courage to assume two distinct speculative positions – a forward-forward and a spot. Instead he fudged them both into one straight forward deal. He simply sold kroners forward for dollars at a discount of 20 per cent (at an annual rate). Suppose further that a 10 per cent devaluation had occurred at the close of business that same day. His realized profit would have netted to near 5 per cent at an annual rate and been payable in three months. If instead the dealer had been intrepid enough both to sell the kroner spot and sell kroners forward one week plus re-purchase them forward three months, his profits would have neared 15 per cent. He would have earned 10 per cent on the spot position. The next day the three-month forward discount would have narrowed to near zero as devaluation would no longer be expected. It has happened already. The kroner dealer could then have closed his forward-forward position at a 5 per cent profit.

The kroner speculator earned substantially extra reward (10 per cent) for having estimated precisely the timing of the devaluation and for having acted on that belief. If he had been mistaken in his judgment, he would have made a greater loss than if he had displayed less speculative finesse. Suppose the expected overnight devaluation had not materialised. He would have borne more than the cost of the overnight forward discount. He would have suffered also a loss on closing the forward-forward position because the three-month discount on the kroner would have widened. The chance of devaluation occurring within three months increases as each day passes and so does the forward discount.

Most foreign exchange dealers prefer the safer life of taking a straight forward position or equivalent rather than trying to win the Royal Flush of the currency game. A Royal Flush is the top winning for trading in a restricted currency that is for long periods pegged to another by official intervention.

Nature laughs at those who would defy it. A central bank which intervenes heavily and restricts trade in its currency market transforms it into the casino of the foreign exchanges. The most rakish elements of the currency game move into the marketplaces where speculators are scorned by officialdom who reject the free determination of the exchange rate.

ODD-DATE TRADING

Secondary market dealing in restricted currencies is hampered by the characteristic volatility of their forward premiums (or discounts). The proposition is illustrated with the example of a trader who starts by selling kroners three months forward for dollars on 1 June at a discount of 10 per cent per annum. By 8 June the three-month discount has widened to 20 per cent and the trader wishes to close his position. He must buy kroners forward for delivery on 1 September, now become an odd-date.

Most forward exchange dealing is for multiples of whole months ahead. Market-makers approached for an odd-date quote anticipate normally matching it with a non-identical maturity. They would have to wait a long time to be bid for another forward contract maturing on the same date. The forward rate may have moved considerably when the bid is received.

The market-making practice of mismatching maturities is described technically as 'gapping'. The risk of loss incurred from gapping is greater where the relation between forward quotes of differing maturity–the forward-forward rates–are volatile. The bid-offer spreads quoted on odd-date forward deals therefore tend to be disproportionately large on restricted currencies compared to freely tradable ones. The kroner dealer would find completing a transaction for 1 September delivery expensive in terms of transaction costs. He would try to delay closing his position until 1 July, when a two-month forward purchase of kroners would be made. The same difficulty of effecting odd-date transactions is experienced in dealing in small tradable currencies where interest and forward rates are volatile.

BEWARE OF THE BEAR SQUEEZE

Speculating in currencies of restricted tradability is hazardous. The speculator there assumes additional risk to that of economic developments differing from expectation. He is also exposed to the danger of a bear squeeze–an official intervention tactic designed to inflict heavy losses on the currency short-seller.

BERLIN SQUEEZE, 1894

The first bear squeeze was operated by the Russian government in 1894. Considerable speculative short-selling of rubles had developed on the Berlin Bourse. The Czar's Minister of Finance, Witte, ordered his agents in Berlin to buy large amounts of ruble notes for forward delivery. Then Witte forbade suddenly the export of ruble notes from Russia. It was physically impossible for all short-sellers of rubles to honour their forward contracts. Russian official forward purchases had amounted to many times the number of ruble notes outside Russia. The ruble short-sellers were at Witte's mercy. He authorised finally the export of extra rubles, but at an artificially high price.

The technique used by Witte is well-known to the organisers of commodity futures exchanges. They have designed rules to prevent any market under their supervision being cornered. Outstanding contracts are monitored to ensure that no operator, directly or indirectly, has a long position of more than a fixed limit. Even so charges of price manipulation in commodity markets are sometimes made. An operator in plywood futures in Chicago might have achieved a long position greater than available stocks of plywood in the vicinity. If he insists on physical delivery on maturity of his contracts, skyrocketing prices would result. Sudden price explosions in any futures market usually cause exchange officials to investigate whether cornering has occurred.

A MODERN BEAR SQUEEZE

In recent years a main user of the bear squeeze tactic has been the Bank of England. The Bank has developed a less extreme form of implementation than Witte's, but its purpose has been the same. By inflicting large losses on short-sellers of sterling (bears) UK officials have hoped to discourage them from ever taking a short position in the future. It is a source of pleasure in the castle of power that those who dared to question the official view of the correct exchange rate should suffer.

The method of operating the UK-type of bear squeeze has been to buy pounds spot and simultaneously to sell them forward. The spot purchase pushes up the spot pound rate and inflicts an immediate loss on bears who were shorting pounds overnight. The forward sale of pounds widens the discount on forward pounds. That reaction is sharp because the forward pound price – like the forward kroner – is subject to only a weak pull of gravity from the domestic credit market. Exchange restrictions limit covered arbitrage between domestic pounds, euro-dollars and the forward pound market.

The widened forward discount on pounds discourages new bears from shorting pounds. Some old bears may salvage a profit from the wrecks of the squeeze. A dealer who had sold pounds forward three months just before the Bank intervened may find that the widening of the three-month discount is greater than the appreciation of the spot rate. A profit is then realized on closing the forward pound position. The gain on the forward-forward component of the three-month forward deal is greater than the loss on the overnight component.

The danger of a bear squeeze increases further the risks of playing for the Royal Flush in the currency game. The player must not only sell the suspect currency overnight, but must complete also a forward-forward transaction. He sells it forward one week and re-buys it three months forward. The bear squeeze causes the player to lose heavily on both positions.

In reality the bears attacked are koala, not grizzly. Exchange restrictions prevent them from borrowing domestic pounds. Instead they borrow euro-pounds to sell spot for dollars. The transaction does not effect the spot pound-dollar exchange rate because of the essential satellite nature of the euro-pound market. Euro-pounds are satellite to the euro-dollar, forward and spot dollar-pound markets. The dealer approached by the sterling bear sells dollars spot for pounds to lend as euro-pounds: he hedges exchange risk by selling pounds forward for dollars. The bear's spot sale of pounds cancels the spot purchase of the dealer. The sum of the bear's and dealer's transaction equals a simple forward sale of pounds and the spot exchange rate is not affected directly.

Consider a crisis situation where a depreciation of the pound appears imminent. Official support operations are expected to cease. Bears rush to borrow euro-pounds from Paris banks in order to short-sell them. Banks act rarely as market-makers in euro-pounds; business is too thin. In the context of large one-way business, as in a crisis, they are almost certain to act as agents in the satellite creation of euro-pounds. The operations of the bank and bear together amount to a forward sale of pounds for dollars.

Suppose the Bank of England reacts to the crisis by effecting a bear squeeze. The forward leg of that transaction deters speculators from selling forward pounds because their price has been reduced thereby. When official and private forward transactions are combined no net reduction in forward sales is to be expected: official sales replace some private ones. Indeed the Bank risks increasing the net supply of forward pounds. Private speculators may have stopped adding to short positions at a narrower forward discount than that achieved by the official operation. Then the forward intervention component of the bear squeeze undoes some of the support given to the spot exchange rate by the spot component. Euro-pound rates are pushed unnecessarily high and some non-resident held domestic pounds are switched to Paris. The increased convenience rent on London pounds discourages their retention. The transfer of pounds from London to Paris causes downward pressure on the spot pound exchange rate (see Chapter 3, p. 71).

The bear squeeze analysis has been cast in terms of the pound market. Similar tactics have been used by other central banks issuing currencies of restricted tradability. In the summer of 1976 the National Bank of Belgium pushed three-month euro-convertible franc interest rates up to 25 per cent per annum by buying francs spot and selling them three months forward. Domestic (and financier) three-month franc rates never exceeded 15 per cent during the crisis.

The impact of bear squeezes is often greatest in the very short-term maturity money market. During a squeeze at the end of May 1977 the Bank of England pushed the one-week euro-pound rate to 13 per cent per annum when the domestic one-week rate was only 8 per cent per annum. The forward leg of the squeeze was effected evidently in the one-week pound exchange market.

Like its Russian ancestor the modern bear squeeze is aimed at short-sellers in a foreign centre. It works by creating an artificial currency shortage there and depends on restricting the inflow of new supplies from the domestic market. The squeeze's modern application is normally faulty because external deposit markets in the restricted currency are satellites of the foreign exchange markets. Dealings in the currency are essentially only in forward form outside the domestic market.

SQUEEZING THE DEUTSCHMARK AND GUILDER

It is illuminating to imagine how a squeeze could be applied to the deutschmark, presently a freely tradable currency. Prime market-making exists in euro-deutschmarks. Suppose the Bundesbank wished to resist a bear attack on the deutschmark which emanated from outside Germany. It could prohibit temporarily German banks from supplying funds to the euro-detuschmark market and from increasing deutschmark loans to non-residents.

The two prohibitions would deter foreign bears because euro-deutschmark interest rates would shoot up. The Bundesbank could act further by itself borrowing euro-deutschmarks, pushing euro-deutschmark rates to still higher levels. Potential short-sellers of deutschmarks are choked off and the spot deutschmark exchange rate steadied. Short-sales of euro-deutschmarks affect the spot deutschmark rate because euro-deutschmarks (unlike euro-pounds) are 'genuine' deposits rather than satellites of the forward deutschmark market. Alternatively the Bundesbank could buy deutschmarks spot and sell them forward having the identical effect to borrowing euro-deutschmarks.

The technical operation of a squeeze on the guilder would differ from the deutschmark example. The euro- and domestic guilder markets are associates of each other. Suppose the Dutch authorities react to a bear raid on their currency by prohibiting resident banks from switching domestic guilders to the euro-guilder market or lending guilders to non-residents. Euro-guilder rates would shoot up and deter some short-selling.

Business in euro-guilders is narrow. The official restrictions placed on arbitrage between euro- and domestic guilders would reduce the euro-guilder market to satellite status. Previous independent market-makers in euro-guilders would find that the loss of associate business from the domestic market makes their activity unprofitable. They find that it is cheaper to manufacture euro-guilders by broking between the dollar-guilder exchange and euro-dollar markets. Unlike the Bundesbank the Dutch Central Bank could not tighten the squeeze by borrowing its euro-currency. The metamorphosis of the euro-guilder into a satellite would make such action as powerless as British authorities borrowing euro-pounds.

In both the German and Dutch examples the bear squeeze is extremely short-term in nature. Over the longer term non-bank residents and non-residents would switch maturing domestic deposits from the domestic to the euro-market. Without instituting a complex control procedure it is feasible to restrict only interbank arbitrage operations between the euro- and domestic market in the currency. Banks may also be requested not to accommodate clients who wish to borrow to undertake arbitrage operations.

FORWARD EXCHANGE INTERVENTION

Forward exchange intervention is not a policy tool exclusive to the central banks of currencies whose tradability is restricted. It has been used in various forms by the Dutch and Swiss central bank as an instrument of domestic credit policy.

The Dutch central bank's foreign exchange intervention assumes most often the form of swap operations. It buys guilders spot and sells them forward (or conversely) and so widens (or narrows) the forward discount on guilders against dollars. The central bank has a target for the forward discount and continues swap operations to resist a narrowing tendency. By setting the discount the bank determines indirectly the level of guilder interest rates. The credit demand of arbitragers pushes up guilder interest rates both in the euro- and its associate domestic Dutch money market, to the new covered parity level with euro-dollar rates.

Official swaps are an instrument of exchange rate, money supply and interest rate policy. If the central bank purchased simply spot guilders for dollars, it would alter the exchange rate and money supply, but have only indirect effect on the level of interest rates. A swap influences directly interest rates by creating increased demand for guilder-denominated credit by arbitragers.

Swaps act directly on credit conditions in the euro-market which then influences the domestic credit market. In the Dutch example the domestic guilder market is an associate of the domestic market and thus the distinction of the location of impact is not important. Suppose however that the Bundesbank conducted official swaps in the dollar-deutschmark market. The euro- and domestic deutschmark markets are not integrated but are separately independent. As explained in Chapter 2 (p. 61) differential reserve requirements on non-resident deposits with banks in West Germany cause domestic deutschmark interest rates to be often greater than covered parity level with euro-dollars. Covered interest arbitrage occurs unrestricted between euro-deutschmarks and euro-dollars.

The Bundesbank swaps have their first impact in the euro-deutschmark market where interest rates are driven up by the force of credit demand of arbitragers. Domestic deutschmark rates would respond only when the euro-deutschmark rate had surpassed them thereby igniting arbitrage credit flows from the domestic to euro-deutschmark market.

The Bundesbank could influence domestic deutschmark rates more directly by operating in the Frankfurt credit market. Domestic rates would be pulled up to the target level by the Bundesbank offering to borrow any funds offered to it at that rate. The monetary implication of the borrowing would be equivalent to that of an equal amount of swap intervention. Both have identical effects on the supply of high-powered money.

Swaps would be an inefficient tool of domestic credit policy in the US for similar reasons to those in Germany. Arbitrage is not perfect between euro- and domestic dollars due to Federal Reserve regulations. Swap operations would be further confounded by the giant size of the euro-dollar market relative to other euro-currency markets. By setting a forward discount against say the deutschmark and Swiss franc, the Fed. could not predict the level of euro-dollar rates. Covered interest arbitrage credit flows from the euro-dollar market would be so large relative to the euro-deutschmark and euro-franc markets that interest rates would be altered there. If the Fed. wishes to determine a target level of domestic dollar rates, it should operate in the domestic dollar credit market.

OFFICIAL FORWARD SWISS FRANC INTERVENTION

Although the Swiss franc is freely tradable various restrictions limit the inflow of non-resident funds into domestic Swiss franc deposits. Further Swiss residents are constrained from borrowing foreign currency or euro-Swiss francs to switch into domestic investments. The Swiss National Bank has conducted swaps – buying francs spot and selling them forward or conversely – for these purposes.

Firstly swaps have been used as an instrument of monetary policy. The Swiss National Bank cannot use the tool of open market operations in the government securities market because there is no domestic money or Treasury Bill market in Switzerland. The market in state bonds is extremely narrow. Yet the National Bank wishes to differentiate between foreign exchange intervention and monetary policy. It does that by operating in the forward Swiss franc market in the opposite direction to its spot intervention. That dampens some of the exchange rate effect of the official spot foreign exchange transactions. The official forward operations do not cancel entirely the spot rate effect because the foreign exchange market in francs is sufficiently large in size relative to the franc denominated credit market for franc interest rates to shift under the pressure of covered interest arbitrage flows.

Secondly swaps have been used as an instrument of credit policy. Swiss banks keep liquid reserves in the euro-Swiss franc market as no interbank market functions domestically. At the end of each month banks must meet liquidity ratios specified usually in terms of deposits with the Swiss National Bank. A tendency develops at end-month for banks to pull in euro-Swiss franc deposits to meet their legal reserve requirements at the Bank. The Bank will sometimes relieve temporary tightness so caused in the euro-franc market by selling francs spot for dollars and buying them back forward. The swap has a similar effect to lending euro-francs. Then private arbitragers would sell francs spot and buy them forward to exploit the resulting covered interest margin between euro-dollar and euro-franc interest rates. In practice the National Bank has never lent euro-francs directly.

Thirdly the National Bank has employed swaps to fight bull speculation from abroad. The operation is a mirror image of the bear squeeze described in the pound market. Suppose the Bank wishes to resist foreign speculative pressure without altering its domestic credit policy. It creates an artificial glut of francs in foreign centres and prevents a re-flow of francs back to Switzerland. Short-term bull speculators suffer losses as the exchange rate falls. The cost of running bull positions is increased greatly as euro-franc rates have collapsed and the premium on forward francs has shot up.

Technically the Bank sells francs spot for dollars and buys them back forward thereby driving down euro-franc interest rates. The lower level of euro-rates discourages foreigners from purchasing francs to place in the euro-market. Further non-residents cannot place large franc deposits with domestic Swiss banks without becoming subject to a barrage of penalties.

The swap tactic for fighting bulls is more efficient than straight spot intervention. The Swiss National Bank, by acting directly on euro-franc rates, deters non-resident uncovered Swiss franc purchases that otherwise would have occurred. If intervention was in the spot market only, the National Bank would merely sell francs to meet speculative demand. In no way is that demand itself reduced directly. Sometimes the swap tactic has driven euro-franc rates to negative levels for short maturities.

Like a bear squeeze a bull attack depends on cutting off the foreign pool of currency from the domestic. Further the external deposit market must be prime supporting independent market-making. Otherwise the bull attack's impact is on the forward rather than spot market. The operation succeeds for Swiss francs because the euro-franc market is prime, not satellite.

INTERNATIONAL MONETARY SYSTEMS

Nearly thirty years elapsed after the Second World War before the free float gained respectability for more than the exceptional central bank. The monetary system built at Bretton Woods was one of fixed exchange rates. Exchange market stabilisation was the function of the central bank. The International Monetary Fund (IMF) was fashioned by men who feared that the international capital market would not revive. The problem was how to prevent governments resorting to trade restrictions or competitive devaluation to bridge trade deficits. It seemed inconceivable that the 'invisible hand' could remedy imbalances in the marketplace.

The architects of the IMF would not have disputed that in a free currency market exchange rate movements could potentially equalise supply and demand. It was believed however that in the uncertain aftermath of the war risk premiums demanded by speculators could be large and exchange rate movements volatile. Evidence was drawn from the experience of floating exchange rates in the 1930s. A skilful advocate for their defence would have countered that currency instability was merely a symptom of political trauma: the US dollar quote of European currencies during the 1930s was a barometer which registered the periodic amassing and dispersal of war clouds.

Having decided to reject floating exchange rates the founders of the IMF diagnosed correctly that the conditions for self-supporting fixed exchange rates did not exist. A fixed parity surviving without official intervention is not impossible where the market has enough confidence in the permanence of a fixed rate–such as that between the Belgian and Luxembourg franc. But this is an exception rather

than the rule in the international arena. So the IMF was to be a
lender of last resort in the defence of fixed parities. A central bank
would turn to it for assistance when the consistency of its monetary
policy with the present exchange rate was doubted by the market.

The edifice of fixed exchange rates collapsed in August 1971 when
the Americans closed the gold window. Cracks had been appearing
in the Bretton Woods system for many years. Any amount of re-
papering could not prevent their re-emergence. The common
source was a failure to coordinate national monetary policies.
Governments sterlised their money supplies from the influence of
money flows across the foreign exchanges impeding the automatic
adjustment mechanism of a fixed exchange rate system.

CODE FOR FLOATING

Despite the abandonment of fixed rates August 1971 was a false
dawn for freely floating exchange rates. Although the major
currencies have floated for most of the period since that date
intervention by national monetary authorities has been persistent
and sometimes massive.

The IMF's reaction to the changed financial environment has
been to seek powers to police the manipulation of exchange rates.
Member agreement was obtained at the Jamaica meeting of
January 1976. The Second Amendment of the IMF charter sets out
the new authority in Article 4. The detailed new code of conduct for
application of Article 4 was confirmed by the Interim Committee of
the IMF in May 1977.

The IMF's metamorphosis into the overseer of the world's
exchange markets has given it a firmer hand over the currency
policies of members. This will help to ensure that governments do
not pursue intervention policies that threaten the survival of
unfettered currency markets. This time the IMF is to be arbiter of
the rules of the game. By contrast in the pre-1971 international
monetary system the Fund had no authority to request members –
unless as a loan condition – to abstain from sterilising international
money supplies.

The Article 4 code contains the following provisions:
1. Members must not manipulate exchange rates in order to
    prevent effective balance of payments adjustment or to gain
    unfair competitive advantage.

2. Members should intervene to correct short-term 'disorderly conditions' in foreign exchange markets.

3. The Fund will be concerned about protracted large-scale intervention in one direction in the exchange market and about signs of an 'unsustainable level of official or quasi-official borrowing for balance of payments purposes'. The behaviour of the exchange rate should be related to underlying economic and financial conditions including factors affecting competitiveness and long-term capital movements.

If the Code is to be enforced effectively, supplementary rule-of-thumb tests need to be developed. For example the ratio of official intervention to private net capital flows would have to be above what figure for it to be assumed 'unsustainable'? Are bear squeezes and bull attacks – both forms of exchange rate manipulation – to be outlawed?

Under Section 2 of the new Article 4 members must notify the Fund within thirty days of ratification of the exchange arrangements which they intend to apply. These are grouped into three categories:

1. Maintenance of an exchange rate in terms of the SDR or another denominator. An example of a currency whose exchange rate is tied to the SDR is the Saudi riyal.

2. Cooperative arrangements by which members maintain the value of their currencies in relation to the value of the currencies of other members, as with the European Snake.

3. Other exchange arrangements of a member's choice.

Category 3 is vague and will presumably be subdivided as experience of operating Article 4 is gained. Some suggested divisions are:

3a A freely floating exchange rate.

3b An adjustable peg with disclosed adjustment formula.

3c An adjustable peg with undisclosed adjustment formula.

3d Systematic intervention in both directions according to a disclosed rule.

3e Sporadic intervention, in both directions, according to a rule known by at most the central bank.

More precise currency defintion allows foreign exchange markets to operate efficiently. Speculators can then base calculation on economic fundamentals rather than guesses about central bank tactics. Exchange market efficiency would be increased further if central banks had to notify the Fund in advance of any switch in currency category. The change in category should also be announced publicly rather than leaving the market to guess for weeks or months whether exchange rate policy has been revised.

The IMF's sanction – the power to withhold cheap finance – would encourage correct registration by central banks. Presumably categories 3c and 3e would be frowned upon and loan covenants would include a clause requiring a change of currency category.

THE IMF AS LENDER

In the pre-1971 system the IMF lent to countries to support a fixed exchange rate on condition that certain adjustment policies were followed. Fixed exchange rates were the essence of the international monetary arrangements of which the IMF was figurehead. In the post-1971 system small currencies are often tied to larger ones, but major currencies are floating. What is the *raison d'être* of IMF lending to 'floaters'?

A main justification must surely be to back provision 2 of the Article 4 code of conduct – to help a member correct short-term 'disorderly conditions' in its foreign exchange market. The attraction of raising IMF finance rather than say euro-borrowing to stabilise an exchange market is its cheapness. The IMF differs from other lenders by including in loan covenants conditions of compliance with its provisions of liberalism in the international economy. By contrast commercial lenders would often be well contented if their sovereign clients imposed trade restrictions as a method of raising foreign exchange.

Disorderly conditions are more likely to occur in the currency markets where tradability is restricted. Where a currency is freely tradable speculators can unhindered absorb excess supplies, or conversely. Further free tradability is associated normally with an 'openness' of the issuing monetary authority, underlying policy stability, and precision in fulfilment of targets. All of these qualities are conducive to low cost speculation. If the IMF persuaded borrowers both to switch from categories 3c and 3e and increase their currency's tradability, it would reduce the need for IMF assistance.

Originally the IMF used to lend to countries to finance an agreed programme of trade liberalisation and the attainment of Article VIII status. Indeed it was this promise that persuaded the US

Congresss to support the creation of the IMF. IMF finance would similarly help achieve the next stage in the realization of the liberal dream – international financial convertibility. Countries would be entitled to assistance for steadying exchange rate adjustment in return for the relaxation of controls. The IMF started life as a torch bearer of liberalism in the international economy. Its mission is far from complete.

5 From Gold to Currency Nationalism

The Tower of Babel of the gold standard world collapsed with the outbreak of war in 1914. Since then the nations of the world have been confounded with many monies. As we expect people in different nations to speak different languages, so we expect them to use different monies. Governments state their laws in the national language. They insist that taxes are paid in the national money.

There is not a one-to-one relationship between languages and states. Three official languages are spoken in Switzerland, two in Canada and Belgium. In the modern generation of states born out of colonies the old imperial language, French or English, is still used widely. The local languages are often not sophisticated enough to express difficult concepts. In Imperial Russia the aristocracy used French rather than the local dialect.

The pattern of money usage is similar to that of language. The wealthy and large corporations see the local money in many countries as unsatisfactory and select assets (and liabilities) denominated in the three major international monies – Swiss francs, West German marks and US dollars. Some countries have chosen not to coin their own money preferring to be part of a larger monetary union. Examples would include Luxembourg and Panama which use the Belgian franc and US dollar respectively. Some have more than one currency in common circulation – for example francs and pesetas in Andorra.

Currency nationalism is more virulent than language nationalism. Few nations care whether their language is used by others; indeed it is recognised as a source of trade benefit. Concern that subjects should communicate only in the official language is associated particularly with new or changed sovereignty. In contrast many nations root out zealously the use of foreign monies within their political jurisdiction. It is often a subject of deep concern in Finance Ministries that their currency is being used by foreigners.

WALL OF CHINA

The motives that lead governments to interfere with the geographical pattern of their currency usage can be broken into three categories – protectionism, mercantilism and economic nationalism.

CURRENCY PROTECTIONISM

A protectionist central bank considers exchange restrictions as a legitimate tool to direct the exchange rate towards the officially preferred level. The central bank would be reluctant to intervene on the massive scale required by buying or selling its currency in the foreign exchange market. Not only might such intervention threaten its monetary targets; it might also be very costly if the chosen exchange rate proves indefensible.

Currency protectionism is essentially a short-run policy designed to meet what is believed to be a perverse speculative movement. Controls once erected have a tendency however to outlive their immediate cause. Vested interests are created in their continued application.

Examples of protectionism are profuse. In December 1968 De Gaulle introduced wide-ranging controls to halt a run on the French franc. Resident purchases of foreign securities, and loans in francs to non-residents, were severely curtailed. Immediate pressure on the franc was relieved although it was devalued within a year. Controls were relaxed subsequently, but not abolished.

In 1974 Japan took currency protection measures at the advent of the world oil crisis. Permission was withdrawn for foreigners to issue bonds in Tokyo. Limits were set to Japanese holdings of foreign currency balances. By the summer of 1977 Japanese trade was again strongly in surplus and the emergency controls were abolished.

Protectionist tactics can also be used by central banks resisting an appreciation of their currency. The Swiss have erected a barrage of negative interest charges, forced conversions and withholding taxes.

In the dollar crisis of the early 1970s the Bundesbank introduced emergency foreign exchange laws to prevent sharp upward deutschmark appreciation due to what was believed to be temporary speculative pressure.

The array of German controls was formidable. 100 per cent reserve requirements were imposed on non-resident deutschmark deposits in West Germany. Reserves pay no interest. Non-residents were prohibited from purchasing domestic deutschmark bonds of less than four years' maturity. A coupon tax was applied on interest payments to non-residents. German resident corporations were discouraged from borrowing abroad to finance investments inside the Federal Republic. In 1974 controls were substantially relaxed. By 1977 remaining protectionist measures included the coupon tax, a ban on non-resident purchases of short-term bonds and a differential reserve requirement between resident and non-resident interbank deposits.

For a short period in 1973 the Netherlands introduced a control system to limit 'speculative' upward pressure on the guilder. Non-residents could purchase guilder bonds only from other non-residents. Transferability was assisted by the institution of 'O-guilder' accounts. Such accounts with the Dutch resident banks could be held only by non-residents. They could be credited with sale proceeds of guilder bonds and non-residents could purchase guilder bonds from Dutch residents only with O-guilders. O-guilders could be transferred freely between non-residents. O-guilders sold at a premium over the official market guilder exchange rate.

The operation of the O-guilder system was not very successful. Dutch securities are typically in bearer form. It was easy for Dutch residents to export bearer guilder bonds without licence and sell them in a foreign centre to non-residents. The exporter would collect the premium price and bank the proceeds in a foreign account. Thereby the foreign currency would be purchased at a discount below the official market guilder exchange rate. The black-market activity in guilder bonds deprived the protectionist measures of effectiveness.

The administration of protectionist controls is most effective against residents. They can be subjected to penalties for breaking the control regulation. Non-resident transactions are much harder to constrain. Protection designed to prevent a depreciation does not usually infringe free convertibility of the currency for non-residents.

In the French 1968 example foreigners were still free to withdraw franc deposits or to sell francs forward.

The introduction of protectionist controls is particularly hazardous for small countries. There local residents are likely to be much better informed than foreigners about the domestic economy. They should be better placed to make speculative judgments. Foreign press coverage of economic events in small countries is scanty. In contrast events in the three largest economies – the US, Japan and West Germany – are given widespread coverage. The disadvantage of the non-resident trading a major currency is less than for a minor. Protectionist measures in a minor currency market subject it to potentially inferior speculation and exclude some top domestic professional speculators.

MERCANTILISM

A mercantilist central bank restricts currency outflows with the long-run objective of squeezing economic advantage from other countries. By restricting capital outflows, encouraging inflows and the use of foreign currencies to finance credit for exports the object is to boost domestic real wages and employment. If the measures are successful, another country or countries must provide the artificially increased capital inflow and so suffer a reduced level of wages and employment.

There are certain occupations that people prefer not to disclose and at most describe euphemistically. So it is with central banks. They would never admit to being mercantilist and they would always introduce the necessary measures under some other guise. The mercantilist frame is built from the flotsam of successive ebbing protectionist tides.

The process of building a system of currency mercantilism is well demonstrated by the history of UK policy. In its pre-Oil Age era sterling was the subject of repeated crises. The Bank of England reacted by imposing even tighter protectionist controls in each successive crisis. When the immediate crisis passed partial relaxations would be made, but never total. A growingly complex control system emerged which came to be defended on mercantilist grounds. By the mid-1970s labour organisations and other interest groups realised fully the benefits of the mercantilist policy for themselves. Politicans were fearful to act in conflict with those pressure groups. In public and internationally the continued controls were justified by the claim that the pound was in a perpetual crisis.

The distinction between currency mercantilism and protectionism was recognised implictly by the authors of the capital liberalisation clauses of the Treaty of Rome which set up the EEC. Capital restrictions were divided into four categories: Lists A to D, that were to be liberalised in successive stages.

Lists A and B include broadly direct investment and the purchase and sale of equities. Lists C and D include money and bond market transactions. A and B restrictions are normally mercantilist in intent. Foreign equities and direct investment provide a poor hedge against an expected exchange rate depreciation which is not large. Adverse movement of equity prices and the transaction costs of dealing there may easily eliminate any exchange rate profit.

Most EEC nations have complied with a directive requiring the liberalisation of List A and B capital flows. The effectiveness of currency protection packages at times of crisis is not greatly reduced thereby. A central bank that is genuinely tackling immediate speculative flows should be content to use List C and D restrictions. They attack the assumption of pure exchange risk positions which must be assumed in foreign bond and money markets. The exclusion of List A and B restrictions ensures the outlawing of mercantilist investment policies.

NATIONALISM

Anthropologists tell us how basic is Man's desire to seek shelter from the harshness of the environment. The same desire finds collective expression in currency politics. Countries may for example try to prevent their currencies being drawn into a whirlwind springing up round the US dollar. Their actions may take two forms described here as strong and weak nationalism.

Weak form nationalism describes the policy of restricting non-residents from either borrowing or lending the currency. West German currency management has been characterised by a weak form nationalism. Certain impediments exist to non-resident investments in the German bond and money markets. The Bundesbank has also attempted to slow the growth of euro-markets in the deutschmark. The issue of bonds by non-residents has been subject to official quotas.

Strong form nationalism describes the placing of restrictions not only on non-residents in their borrowing and lending the local currency but also on residents borrowing and lending foreign currencies. The Bank of Japan's currency policy fitted the description until Spring 1977. Non-resident purchases of yen bonds were impeded. The growth of a foreign yen bond market was resisted. Japanese residents had to obtain permits to either borrow or purchase foreign currencies. Mercantilism was not evident. No restrictions prevented the Japanese from making direct or equity investments overseas. Foreigners were free to make direct or equity investments in Japan.

Nationalism can be distinguished easily from protectionism. Measures taken under the banner of nationalism lack directional bias. If they were undone, it should be unclear whether the exchange rate would depreciate or appreciate. Nationalism describes usually a long-term policy not one designed to meet a short-term crisis.

WHERE NOW?

Currency politics are volatile. Still some insight may be gained from labelling central bank policies as at Spring 1977. The exercise is completed in Table 5.1.

TABLE 5.1   Central bank politics

	Protectionism	Mercantilism	Nationalism
US dollar	No	No	No
West German mark	No	No	Mild
Swiss franc	Yes	No	Mild
Japanese yen	No	No	Mild
French franc	Mild	No	No
British pound	Strong	Strong	No

BORROWING ASYMMETRY

Restrictions on foreign borrowing in domestic capital markets are pervasive. Both the Dutch central bank and the Bundesbank for example ration bond issues by non-residents in their domestic capital market. Their motive appears to be to insulate the domestic interest rate structure from external influences.

Suppose deutschmark bond yields were low relative to dollar bond yields, given general expectations of the likely dollar-deutschmark exchange rate movement. Germans would tend to switch to holding more dollar bonds. The switch would be limited due to their unwillingness to assume foreign exchange risk. Foreign corporations would see a favourable opportunity to issue bonds denominated in deutschmarks rather than dollars. Although each foreign corporation would be reluctant to increase greatly the currency risk of its borrowing, their combined borrowing could be large relative to the size of the domestic bond market. The new issues would drive up yields in the deutschmark bond market and be purchased primarily by German residents. They assume no exchange risk in buying foreign deutschmark bonds. German purchases of these issues represents a capital outflow from Germany.

A greater German demand for foreign bonds results from the initial deutschmark-dollar bond yield discrepancy, than if all foreign investments involved exchange risk for the capital exporter. Hence foreign access to the local bond market exposes yields there more to international influences. The exchange risk which must be borne when capital flows internationally between bond markets can be widely dispersed in both resident and non-resident portfolios.

A small capital market like the Dutch would be particularly exposed to international developments. A small change in the amount of guilder borrowing by foreign corporations could burst the dyke built out of local aversion to exchange risk. The Dutch bond market would be swamped by the borrowing operations of multinationals.

Currency nationalists fear foreign investment as much as foreign borrowing in the domestic bond market, especially where it is small. Suppose that guilder bond yields were high relative to dollar bond yields given exchange rate expectations. Then foreign demand could flood the Dutch bond market even though non-residents made only slight changes to the currency composition of their portfolios.

Foreign borrowers and lenders in a domestic bond market are normally the most influenced by exchange rate expectations. Few of them earn a convenience return from denominating borrowing or lending in the local currency. So internationalisation would increase the exposure of domestic yields to international influences. The exception is where the local currency has achieved the status of a widely used international unit of account in which many non-residents dream. They too earn convenience return from using the local unit.

WHEN NEW YORK OPENS

At 2 p.m. each business day Europe trembles. How will the opening of the American markets affect commodity and currency prices? Market sentiment can vary markedly between Europe and the US. Europe might be bearish and the US bullish on the dollar. A tendency would then be observed for the dollar to fall in Europe during its morning to be pulled back by New York in the afternoon.

Currency nationalists dislike their money's exchange rate or interest rate being deflected by foreign market sentiment which differs from domestic. They would build a barrier to separate the external from the domestic markets.

MARKET ECLIPSE

When two markets are open simultaneously it is not possible to identify differential market sentiment between the two. Arbitragers ensure that the same commodity or currency is traded at the same price in the two centres. Sentiments can be distinguished between markets in two instances; first when their trading times are not synchronised, second when restrictions permit a margin of tolerance by which prices can differ between two markets.

Some speculators specialise in spotting differential market sentiment. A copper trader in London may believe that prices have opened too low because the market is bullish on pounds and participants are reluctant therefore to take long positions in pound denominated forward contracts. He expects that the New York opening price will be higher and that arbitrage between London and New York will then drive up the London price. So he assumes a long position in the London forward contract in the morning, hoping to close at a profit that same day.

On 1 January 1975 the US gold market re-opened after 42 years of slumber. During the preceding months Europe and Asia

speculated on what sentiment America would display towards the
yellow metal. In the event America proved to be much less keen on
gold investment than was anticipated.

Paris was most bullish on gold as can be deduced from the relative
price behaviour there compared to other centres. The import and
export of gold from France is restricted so that perfect arbitrage is
impossible. The premium of the Paris gold price over the world
price widened to 5 per cent by 31 December 1974, indicating the
degree of French bullishness. Table 5.2 displays how the Paris gold
premium moved during two months in the winter of 1976.

TABLE 5.2   Paris gold market

	Francs/$	Paris gold price francs/ kilo	Paris gold price $/oz	London gold price $/oz	Premium of Paris over London price
1976					
30 Jan.	4·477	18·900	131·32	128·15	2·47
6 Feb.	4·471	19·500	135·65	130·60	3·86
13 Feb.	4·464	19·450	135·52	131·10	3·37
20 Feb.	4·473	19·250	133·84	131·75	1·58
27 Feb.	4·489	19·310	133·78	132·30	1·11
5 Mar.	4·513	19·495	134·34	133·70	0·47

Differential market sentiment is highlighted sometimes during
currency crises. Bresciani-Turroni, in his chronicle of the German
hyperinflation of 1921–3, recounts how Berlin was more bearish
than New York. The origin of sharp depreciations of the mark was
the Berlin Bourse where the quotations were generally more
favourable than in New York. The mark tended to rise there after
Berlin closed.

Europe led the way during the dollar fall in mid-summer 1977.
Foreign exchange dealers had sensed for weeks that short dollar
positions were being built up in European centres. On 4 July the US
markets were closed for Independence Day. The dollar was marked
down when Europe opened. A further decline set in which could not
be halted as normally from New York. By the next afternoon, when
New York opened eventually, the lower dollar quote had become
established.

Some Canadian commentators saw the Chicago IMM as the

culprit for the plummeting of the Canadian dollar in Spring 1977. It is true that IMM turnover in the Canadian dollar contract rose sharply. The Canadian dollar displaced the egg futures market from its trading pit on the floor of the mercantile exchange. It was impossible however to prove that a predominance of bears were to be found in Chicago. IMM trading hours were coincidental with other major currency markets in North America. Indeed increased volume could have been due to hedging, arbitrage or speculative operations in either direction.

INTERPRETING INTEREST MARGINS

Arbitrage is not perfect either between the euro-dollar and domestic US money market or between the euro-deutschmark and domestic German money market. Yet the euro-domestic interest rate differential for both can move only within a narrow band. At any point in time the size of the differential compared to its possible maximum and minimum is an indicator of how far market sentiment differs in foreign and domestic centres.

Non-resident interbank deutschmark deposits in Germany are subject to a 10 per cent reserve requirement: resident interbank deposits are exempt. Interest rates on euro-deutschmarks can therefore be up to 10 per cent below those in Frankfurt without arbitrage profit being exploitable. Interest rates on the euro-deutschmark cannot rise above the Frankfurt level because arbitrage would then be immediate. If interest rates on deutschmarks in Luxembourg fall from 5 per cent to 10 per cent below Frankfurt, it can be deduced that either foreigners have become more bullish than the Germans about the deutschmark or that foreign demand for deutschmark credit is relatively sluggish.

US reserve requirements are structured differently from the German. They apply equally to resident and non-resident deposits with US domestic banks. US reserve requirements apply also to the issue of domestic dollar CDs. In consequence euro-dollar rates could not fall below equivalent maturity US money market rates. US banks would then make arbitrage profits from borrowing dollars in Europe and lending them domestically. Euro-dollar rates cannot rise more than a fixed margin—determined by reserve requirements—above US dollar rates. Then US banks would arbitrage by borrowing in the US and re-lending in Europe.

Only Federal funds borrowing is exempt from reserve requirements. Federal funds borrowing by US domestic banks is almost entirely overnight. Arbitrage tends to equate overnight euro-dollar and Federal funds rates. A narrow market exists in 'term Federal Funds' for longer maturities. It is an associate market of the much broader euro-dollar market and is used often by Canadian banks for covered arbitrage operations between US and Canadian dollars.

When dollar interest rates are around 6 per cent US dollar CD rates can be as much as one-half percentage point below euro-dollar CD rates without profitable arbitrage being possible. Movements of the US dollar-euro-dollar CD rate differential between 0 and $\frac{1}{2}$ per cent indicate relative credit pressures in Europe and the US. During the Spring of 1977 the CD rate differential was frequently at its maximum for three-month maturities. Not only was Europe more bearish about the dollar, but it was also more fearful of an imminent tightening of Federal Reserve monetary policy and a rising level of dollar interest rates. There was a pronounced tendency for dollar interest rates to open high in London and to be pulled back in the afternoon. Banks could speculate by lending euro-dollars in London's morning hoping to reverse at a profit in the afternoon when the weight of bullish US sentiment would be felt.

CUCKOO CLOCK PROTECTION

Switzerland has two traditional export industries – the cuckoo clock and bank services. Both enjoy a degree of official protection. In Table 5.1 the policy of the Swiss National Bank was described as mildly nationalistic. A prime motive for its regulations in the Swiss franc market is the desire to protect the profits of Swiss banks rather than overt nationalism.

The National Bank prides itself on having managed a currency that has now the reputation of being the most stable. Currencies cannot be patented. In order to ensure that profits from developing their 'product' accrue to Switzerland the National Bank has tried to impede the growth of an external Swiss franc market. It has prevented successfully the formation of a euro-bond market denominated in Swiss francs. Yet the National Bank has sponsored a foreign franc bond market in Switzerland of major importance. The market is in private placements and foreign companies are estimated to have raised there 10 bn francs in 1976. Today the franc private placements market is one of the most important single sources of international capital. Interest on these foreign bonds is exempt from withholding tax. Exemption is essential if they are to compete successfully with other money brands of international bonds. In contrast to euro-bonds foreign Swiss franc bonds are issued and traded in only one country, Switzerland. Swiss banks are thereby assured 100 per cent of the brokerage revenues.

THE PRICE OF STABILITY

Switzerland has the reputation of being the safest abode in the world for savings. Bank secrecy is enforced strictly. The Swiss Government, in addition to the Swiss banking industry, derives direct revenue from providing these services.

Withholding tax is charged on interest from domestic Swiss securities. Foreign purchases of Swiss cantonal bonds demonstrate the significance of political stability. Cantonal bonds yield on average a half to one percentage point less than equal maturity foreign franc bonds. Investors are prepared evidently to accept an inferior return and pay withholding tax in order to include Swiss names in their portfolios. They believe that Swiss cantons will still pay interest on their bonds even in the event of world catastrophe. Withholding tax is the price charged for the ultimate guarantee and is paid to the Swiss Government.

SWISS REFUGE

So important is the security of the Swiss name that the domestic and euro-franc money market would be partially segregated even if all official restrictions were removed. Banks in Switzerland would attract franc deposits at a lower rate than banks in London.

Discrimination would occur also in bank lending. Banks – in and outside of Switzerland – would have to charge lower interest rates to Swiss than non-Swiss names of otherwise identical risk. A London bank could not therefore compete with a Swiss bank in lending francs to a Swiss customer. Its borrowing cost would be greater.

When lending francs to non-Swiss names the marginal borrowing costs of the two banks would be closer. Potential depositors with the

Swiss bank would appraise that its credit rating was affected
adversely by the assumption of foreign names in its loan portfolio.
The marginal cost of its borrowing would increase.

Patterns of international trade are determined by comparative,
not absolute, cost advantage. Swiss banks would have a comparative advantage in lending francs to foreigners.

The basis of segregation in the Swiss franc market is the
inequality of residence. A London and Zurich bank with identical
loan portfolios are not of identical risk. The Zurich bank could
attract deposits at a cheaper rate than the London bank. The
natural advantage of the Swiss bank declines as it increases the
proportion of loans to non-Swiss clients. In a world catastrophe—
such as war—a Swiss bank which had lent mainly to foreigners
would be not much safer than a foreign bank. On the other hand a
Swiss bank which had lent predominantly to Swiss names would be
considerbly safer than a foreign bank which had done the same.
Deposits at the foreign bank could be likely blocked, although its
loans were sound.

SWISS REFLECTIONS

In the inflationary and recessionary storms of the 1970s weary
citizens of the world have sought the sanctuary of Switzerland for
their capital. The Swiss have responded by erecting controls on
inward capital movements into the franc thus insulating it as far as
possible from the outside world. The controls have been partly
protectionist in intent, to stave off an immediate sharp franc
appreciation. The hope was to ease the adjustment of Swiss export
industries to inevitable franc strength. The longer term justification
was nationalist: to shelter the franc from fluctuations attributable to
changing foreign sentiment. Controls were also introduced to
smooth the outflow of francs into foreign bond issues denominated
in francs.

THE CONTROL SYSTEM

Regulations change frequently yet the underlying principles remain
steady. Non-resident franc deposits with domestic banks are subject
to negative interest charges, if over 250,000 francs. Swiss residents

may not borrow abroad with the intent of using the proceeds to invest in Switzerland. Banks incur penalties if they have a net long position in domestic francs. Non-residents are circumscribed in their purchase of Swiss real estate.

Borrowing by foreigners in Swiss francs is controlled. A monthly quota is fixed by the National Bank for public issues of foreign franc bonds. All franc credits to foreigners, and all proceeds from foreign bond issues in Switzerland, must be converted immediately into foreign currency at the Swiss National Bank. The objective is to smooth flows through the franc exchange market. The Bank resells the francs in the exchange market over longer periods of time consistent with its stabilisation objectives. The Bank has further forbidden Swiss banks from participating in Swiss franc denominated syndicated credits – hoping to limit the use of the franc in LDC financing.

The structure of the Swiss equity market is two-tiered. Corporations issue registered and bearer shares. The bearers sell at a premium and reportedly are bought largely by non-residents. They do not wish normally to buy registered shares because of possible tax and legal complications. Sometimes foreigners are ineligible to purchase registered shares. They are bought primarily by the Swiss and a higher yield is obtainable on them than on the bearer shares.

BEARER SECURITIES

It has already been described here how the export of bearer shares from the Netherlands defeated the attempt to protect the guilder from capital inflows. The Swiss do not face the same difficulty. There is no bill market in Switzerland and the bond markets are narrow. Banks are not permitted to issue certificates of deposit (CDs). Bearer CDs would of course defeat the control authorities. As the holder would be unknown it would be impossible to distinguish residents and non-residents.

Bearer equities and cantonal bonds can be purchased by foreigners. But bearer equities are in limited supply and a premium is effectively paid by the non-resident. Cantonal bonds are lower-yielding than foreign franc bonds and are subject to tax. They form the foundation of non-resident portfolios rather than the trading portion. Foreign franc bonds are in bearer form but their issue and conversion is controlled tightly. The National Bank discourages the formation of secondary markets in foreign franc bonds, fearing greater resulting volatility of the exchange rate and franc interest rates. Investment in foreign franc bonds tends therefore to be essentially long-term. The organisation of the franc market is designed to reduce short-run speculative movements and so partially insulate the domestic market from external influences.

The National Bank's influence extends beyond Switzerland. It has prevented successfully the growth of a franc CD market both at home and abroad. In theory London banks could issue and make a market in franc-CDs. Such a development would accelerate the internationalisation of the franc as the forms in which it could be held became more attractive. The National Bank has made known its objection. A bank which proceeded regardless would find business difficult in Switzerland or with Swiss banks.

Similar deterrents prevent the emergence of a euro-bond market denominated in francs. The placing power of Swiss banks is so important that issue of any euro-bond is difficult without their cooperation. A franc denominated euro-bond issue would be boycotted and consequently fail. The extra-legal power that deters internationalisation belongs to the species exercised by a cartel against recalcitrants.

The National Bank's control network has hardly impinged on the growth of the euro-franc deposit market. The Bank has requested Swiss banks periodically not to increase loans and deposits in francs through their foreign branches. But foreign subsidiaries of Swiss banks have no comparative advantage in euro-franc dealing. The euro-franc market is sufficiently broad to support independent market-making by many banks. To the extent that Swiss subsidiaries curtail their euro-franc activities the business is gained simply by non-Swiss competitors.

Swiss National Bank figures released in Spring 1977 estimated the size of the euro-franc money market at Sw.fr. 40 billion. Euro-francs are genuine deposits and not satellite to the forward franc market; business is sufficiently deep to support independent market-making. Foreign purchase of euro-francs hence puts upward pressure on the spot franc exchange rate. The pressure is reduced by euro-franc interest rates falling rapidly: controls on arbitrage prevent their being steadied by the domestic franc credit market.

RISING CURRENCIES OF THE ORIENT

The process of growth of the international use of a currency has similarities with that of language. The Swiss franc in the world of currencies is the equivalent of French in the world of languages. Both enjoy popularity internationally because of their refinement and excellence of expression. The Swiss have an unmatched reputation for monetary management.

The US dollar is the equivalent of English. For most nationals English is the tongue known to most foreigners they are likely to meet. Economy is gained in learning languages if everyone specialises in English. A Dane may well communicate with a Dutchman in English rather than either wasting resources on having learnt Danish or Dutch in addition to English. Transaction costs are saved by non-US businessmen denominating international trade in US dollars. A Swedish exporter to the UK will often denominate his contract in dollars. As a large proportion of world trade is with the US, and the dollar exchange markets are the broadest, the dollar's use has spread to third party trade.

The pivotal role of the US dollar in currency markets was described in Chapter 2 (p. 43). Exchange markets between non-dollar currencies are satellite to dollar-exchange markets. No economy would result from the Swede invoicing the Englishman in pounds. If the Swede hedged his receipts by selling pounds forward for kroners, the bank would effect two deals – one in forward dollar-pounds and one in forward dollar-kroners – to arrive at its quote. Rather than either party wasting bargaining time on whether the contract should be denominated in kroners or pounds they agree on dollars. Then each completes one leg of the composite forward deal that one would otherwise have had to effect.

Not all foreign trade is hedged in the forward exchange markets. A Hong Kong exporter to Japan may have to order simultaneously imports from Japan. He would agree readily to both being denominated in yen rather than dollars thus saving transaction costs. Currencies of countries which are the focus of regional trade will therefore gain international usage on a regional scale. The yen is second to the US dollar as a denominator in Asian trade; similarly the deutschmark in EEC trade.

No business rules are exact. Though the initial regional growth of yen and deutschmark denomination was for unhedged trade, familiarity bred acceptance for use sometimes when hedging was intended.

CURRENCY NAKEDNESS

The yen's growth as a denominator of Asian trade has been associated with a growth of a forward yen market. Whereas previously a Japanese export to Australia would have been priced in US dollars, now it may be priced in yen; similarly for imports from Australia. The Australian importer or exporter may hedge by a forward yen deal.

The broadening of the yen forward market has reduced bid-offer spreads there. In consequence a euro-yen market has developed in recent years. The market is mainly a satellite of the euro-dollar, spot and forward dollar-yen markets. The lower foreign exchange transaction costs, by bringing the swap points closer together, have lowered dealing costs sufficiently on euro-yen to attract borrowing and lending interest.

The growth of a euro-yen market brings international influences to bear on the domestic yen market. The yen has not yet reached dream status. Non-resident borrowing and lending of the currency is potentially more volatile than domestic being primarily speculative in nature. Two policy responses are possible, one nationalistic, the other internationalist.

The Bank of Japan has chosen so far the nationalistic response. Barriers restrict the flow of funds between euro- and domestic yen. The official intent has been to insulate domestic interest rates and enforce a policy of domestic credit rationing. Commercial banks are presently assigned quotas as to what extent they can increase yen loans to different categories of client. Interest rates are administered rather than market-determined. If flows to and from the euro-yen market were unimpeded, quotas would lose force. Banks would arrange euro-yen loans on similar terms to domestic for clients falling outside the assignment categories. The cobweb of credit controls would be blown away by the fresh air of internationalisation.

The internationalist response to euro-yen growth would be to stimulate the yen's role as an international unit of account hoping to achieve dream status. The Swiss model would act as a balance to the growing speculative flows associated with the broadened forward market. Credit flows motivated by exchange rate considerations would be potentially a smaller proportion of the total yen credit market. Interest rates would become increasingly insulated from exchange market influences.

EURO-PROFIT HANDOUTS

Control systems create pockets of unexploited profit opportunity. Controllers reward their favourites by granting them limited access to their sheltered gardens.

The Japanese authorities permit banks to switch non-resident yen deposits into euro-yen. Domestic yen interest rates are usually lower than euro-yen rates. Further banks are prohibited from paying higher interest rates on non-resident than resident deposits. A rental income can therefore be earned from non-resident deposit business.

UK controllers assign rental income in similar fashion. Each bank is granted a quota limiting the extent to which they can borrow domestic pounds to lend in the euro-pound market. Certain precepts are followed, but the final outcome is negotiable. A running profit from 'switching' between domestic and euro-pounds is one of the budgeted profits of London banks.

SAUDI RIYAL INTERNATIONALISATION

By 1977 the riyal was being used increasingly to denominate Middle East trade and finance. Some of the development occurred naturally as a result of the growing regional trade with Saudi Arabia. Actions taken by the Saudi Government also contributed. It has insisted that all government contracts be denominated in riyals and has encouraged merchants to request that import contracts should be denominated in riyals too. The development of a forward riyal market has thus been stimulated as traders with Saudi Arabia have sought to hedge their contracts. The riyal is freely tradable.

The attitude of the Saudi Government to internationalisation has been schizophrenic. At the same time as encouraging the riyal's use in trade they have limited its use in the international bond markets. Only favoured Arab nations have been able to float riyal bonds. In theory riyal bonds could be issued in centres such as Bahrain or

London without Saudi permission. Bahrain would not however sanction an issue if it was known to be counter to Saudi policy. Bahrain owes its financial existence to the benign neglect of the Saudi Monetary Authority. London dealers are also ill-equipped to flout Saudi rules. They must have access to Saudi riyal loans to finance their inventory of riyal bonds. If the displeasure of the Arabian authorities was incurred, they might be refused permission to borrow riyals.

An external riyal deposit market has developed in Bahrain. Banks there are not subject to reserve requirements on riyal business, unlike inside Saudi Arabia. Saudi banks tend to channel business through their Bahrain associates in order to circumvent Saudi credit directions and other credit regulations. Residents of the Gulf States deal to some extent in riyals as well as in their local currencies.

CURRENCY GEOGRAPHY

The pattern of currency usage shifts more rapidly than that of languages. In the 1930s the two international currencies were the pound and dollar. As 1980 is approached the three established investment currencies are the US dollar, West German mark and Swiss franc. There is only one international trade currency – the US dollar. There are three regional trade currencies – the yen, riyal and deutschmark. Within each region trade use of the dollar still predominates.

Patterns of currency trade use are formed predominantly on the basis of the importance of the issuing country in the international economy. Currency convertibility is also essential. Not all traders wish to hedge by using forward markets which are often narrow. Secondary market dealing is difficult in small or restricted currencies and forward facilities are not available for long maturities. Denominating contracts in a fully convertible currency, combined with financing in the same currency, provides a foreign exchange risk hedge.

Consider a UK manufacturer who has contracted to deliver machinery to a Swedish importer over a five-year period. Suppose that prices over the contract's duration are fixed in Swedish kroners. The UK exporter could not hedge the exchange risk by borrowing kroners over a 0–5 year period. No external kroner market exists and non-Swedes cannot easily borrow kroners domestically in

Sweden. He could hedge on a rollover basis, selling kroners forward three months for pounds and renewing at maturity. The hedge obtained by rollovers is often unsatisfactory because the cost of forward cover on small or restricted currencies is volatile.

The use of a fully convertible currency, such as dollars, solves the hedging problem. Suppose the dollar is the denominator of the contract between the Swede and the Englishman. The UK exporter obtains exchange cover by borrowing dollars; the Swede importer by investment in 0–5 year dollar paper, the maturing proceeds being applied to payment of the Englishman.

A two-way link exists between international investment and trade use of a currency. Trade use promotes forward market development which reduces spreads in the euro-deposit market. Greater trade use is in turn encouraged by development of international credit facilities.

Whether the regional role of the riyal and yen expands will hinge on the progressive removal of barriers to international participation in the respective credit markets. Reduction of transaction costs and the lengthening of maturities in the euro-yen and riyal markets are fundamental to trade popularity. Only the deutschmark satisfies the preconditions for overtaking the US dollar as trade denominator within its region.

ATLAS OF THE WORLD ECONOMY?

'There Atlas, son of great Iapetus,
With head inclined and ever-during arms,
Sustains the spacious heavens'.

Hesiod.

In Greek mythology Zeus punished the giant Atlas by condemning him to hold the world on his broad shoulders. The US dollar can be portrayed as shouldering the international monetary system. The US's role as provider of the dollar is not unambiguously burdensome.

The US is, with minor exceptions, the only state to allow its currency to be freely used in the international economy. The Bundesbank and Swiss National Bank – the issuers of the two other international investment currencies – impose certain limits already discussed on the use of their currency by non-residents.

A NATIONALIST WORLD

To appreciate the role of an international currency it is worthwhile considering what the world would be like without any. Suppose all central banks successfully prevented their residents from lending their currency to non-residents and non-residents from holding it. Each central bank would be described as weak form nationalist, according to the definition developed earlier in this chapter. Each is assumed further to prevent the formation of external (euro-) markets in its currency.

Speculation by government officials or private operators would be impossible in the spot exchange markets. Central banks could neither borrow foreign currencies nor hold them in reserves. Similarly private operators could neither short-sell currencies in short supply nor mop up those in excess supply. All currencies would be freely floating, but the absence of first and second order speculators would cause exchange rate movements to be volatile.

All international investment flows would assume equity form in the world of currency nationalism. A German corporation expanding into the US could not borrow dollars; its subsidiary there would have to be purchased with deutschmarks. Oil sheiks could not invest their revenue in dollar, deutschmark and Swiss franc bond and money instruments. They would be forced into equity and commodity purchases. International institutions such as the World Bank and EEC would be unable to raise finance other than by official subscription. They would be without passport to the only capital markets available – the national ones.

Hedging exchange risk in international trade would often be difficult. Though forward exchange markets would function freely, their maturities would be short and transaction costs high, especially for narrowly traded currencies. It was demonstrated in Chapter 4 how restrictions on arbitrage between the forward currency market and its domestic credit market added to the costs of market-making in forward exchange.

Mercantilism – the policy of extracting advantage at the neighbour's cost – would be less rewarding. The UK during its mercantilist phase of the mid-1970s insisted that overseas investment by its residents be financed by foreign currency borrowing. The purpose was to prevent a net capital outflow lest it reduced local employment and real wages. The policy depended on UK corporations being able to borrow either in other national capital markets or in the international capital market. The latter's importance was demonstrated by the disproportionate share of UK corporate names in the total of euro-bond issues.

LDCs would be cut off from foreign sources of capital because they lack domestic equity markets of consequence. Their trade with the developed world is financed mainly in international currencies; in the nationalist world that would be impossible. Domestic LDC credit markets would in most cases be too narrow to assume the burden of trade financing.

'IF GOD DID NOT EXIST IT WOULD BE NECESSARY TO INVENT HIM' (VOLTAIRE)

If no central bank allowed its currency to be internationalised, an international money would have to be invented. It would most likely be based on gold. Bonds and bills in the international capital markets would be gold-denominated. Gold would come to be used as the international unit of account in trade. As in commodity futures markets, gold contracts would include an option for either party to require delivery of the metal. In no sense would a gold, or gold exchange standard, have so been restored. No central bank would undertake to exchange its currency for gold at a fixed price.

Gold's special features that make it suitable for the base of a monetary system are well-known. Its storage and transport costs are low and huge inventories of the metal exist above ground all over the world. Annual production and industrial use are a very small proportion of the above ground supplies and their influence on the gold price is therefore limited.

How would the interest rate on credit market instruments denominated in gold – designed here 'paper gold' – be determined? The clue is to be found in Chapter 3 where forward and spot pricing of commodities were discussed. The interest rate must be such as to eliminate profitable arbitrage from borrowing in gold (by issuing paper gold), investing the proceeds in an interest-bearing currency deposit and buying gold forward for the maturity of the loan. If physical gold supplies are abundant, the metal's convenience rent is zero and the premium of the forward over spot price equals approximately the local currency interest rate. Such is the forward spot relation in the gold futures market today. The operation of arbitragers would then establish a near zero interest rate on paper gold.

The international monetisation of gold would be likely to cause the convenience rent on physical gold to become positive. Banks in particular would hold some gold in physical form to meet demands for delivery. The interest rate on paper gold – interest is itself payable in paper gold – would equal the convenience rent on the physical metal.

The real price of gold (in terms of a weighted basket of consumer goods) would be much more stable than in the present financial system. The total size of gold holdings, including paper gold, would be many times the present. A much smaller proportion would be held by pure speculators. A larger proportion would be held by 'permanent' investors who dreamt in gold and by those using it for transactions purposes. Transaction costs would be reduced by holding some liquid assets in paper gold. Not only would international trade and credit be denominated in gold, but paper gold bank deposits would also be used as an international means of payment. Paper gold would be the only money in which international institutions could deal and the only foreign money which nationals could hold.

Gold's monetary role would probably be entirely as an international means of payment. The demand for real money balances in gold denomination should be assumed to be as stable as for those in national currency denominations. The monetary demand for paper gold would be a function of the same type of precautionary and transaction variables.

The stabilising effect of the reintroduction of a monetary function for gold on its price can be demonstrated with a hypothetical example. Suppose civil war broke out in South Africa. The real price of gold would tend to rise as fears grew that an important source of new metal would be cut off. An excess supply of real paper gold money balances would result. Yet the supply of paper gold money (in units of gold) would not be affected directly. Banks would have a demand for reserves of physical gold – the high-powered money of the paper gold system – which would bear a steady relation with their paper gold money liabilities. Gold stocks and their proportionate division between banks and non-banks remain substantially unchanged at first, and the excess real paper gold money supply must be balanced by additional real gold money demand for equilibrium to be re-established. Rising gold prices of commodities and national currencies provide the necessary stimulant to monetary paper gold demand. Equivalently the real price of gold must return back towards its original level.

The re-monetisation of gold would reduce also the sensitivity of its price to changes in investment demand. Changes in demand for gold denominated credit would tend to occur simultaneously for two reasons. Firstly gold's popularity as a unit of account would often be symmetric for both lenders and borrowers. Secondly a reduction in the international flow of funds may be the source of both reduced lending and borrowing in gold. An oil price fall of 25 per cent could be the occasion for such a reduction. OPEC demand for paper gold investments and oil consuming countries' demand for paper gold borrowing would fall about equally. Both reasons depend on the use of gold to denominate borrowing which would be symptomatic of its remonetisation.

Central bank borrowing and lending internationally would be in paper gold. Physical gold would not be lent because it provides a convenience return. Governments would hold some inventories of physical gold for reasons of national security. Central banks would hold some physical gold to fulfil a lender of last resort function to the paper gold banking system.

Commercial banks would deal in the local money and paper gold. Protectionist and mercantilist central banks would impede the acquisition by their residents of securities denominated in paper gold. Other central banks would allow free choice between their own money and paper gold; they would hope to sell their own on the strength of its excellence of management and its pervasive use in denominating domestic transactions. Speculation in the local currency would be effected by residents who would either short-sell paper gold to buy it when in glut, or conversely.

CORNERING GOLD

An ever-present danger in any market where short-selling is possible is that the underlying physical commodity will be cornered. One instance was illustrated in Chapter 4 where a central bank would itself corner the currency market to effect a bear squeeze.

A paper gold system can be cornered if large groups of investors in paper gold demand payment in physical gold. Borrowers who had issued gold claims (short-sellers of gold) would be caught in a squeeze. The price of gold would skyrocket as borrowers scrambled to obtain the metal to make delivery on the maturity of their contracts. The convenience rent on physical stocks would shoot up and so would the interest rate on paper gold.

Commodity futures markets attack the cornering problem by limiting the size of long position that can be assumed by any one individual or group acting in concert. In a paper gold system potential cornerers would include central banks and governments. Agreed rules of the game would have to limit their power to make large sudden switches from paper to physical gold.

Central banks would protect their local paper gold markets from being cornered. Suppose French banks found themselves faced with large demands for delivery of metal against their maturing paper gold deposits. The Bank of France would lend physical gold to them in exchange for a paper gold deposit thereby replacing the private deposits being withdrawn.

Many brands of paper gold money would exist. They would be differentiated by the mark of the issuing bank and its political jurisdiction. French paper gold money may be better regarded than German because physical gold reserves in France are known to be much larger. The guarantee of lender of last resort function would be firmer there. The interest rate paid on French paper gold claims would then be a shade lower than on German. The comparative advantage of French banks in the gold money market would be analagous to that of US banks in the euro-dollar deposit market because of their supposed access to Federal Reserve facilities.

In the pre-1914 gold standard world the pound sterling, US dollar and French franc were effectively different brands of paper gold. The pre-1914 system differed from the one described here in the exclusion of parallel major national fiat monies. Investors could not choose between British paper gold and British pounds. They were one and the same. In the hypothetical system described not only would national monies and paper gold be distinct, but their rates of exchange would be freely floating.

GOLDEN OPPORTUNITY MISSED?

The Franco-American battle over the role of gold in the international monetary system raged through the late 60s and early 70s. The US sought the demonetisation of the yellow metal. Under

American auspices the IMF saw as one of its main tasks the expunging of gold from its Articles of Agreement. The task was as mammoth as if the Catholic Church had decided that the word God was to be expunged from the Bible.

In the aftermath of the dollar's final break from gold parity in 1971 currency nationalism became rampant in Europe. The Dutch, Belgian, Swiss, French and German central banks all experimented with new controls on their currency acquisition. It could be argued strongly in that context that a campaign against an obvious candidate international money – gold – was mistaken.

Large gold stocks are held all over the world. Surely it would be an efficient use of world resources to assign gold some function in a monetary system. Either gold is to remain an investment commodity locked in subterranean vaults, or it can be put to use as the base of a monetary system in which it would yield a convenience return.

The problem of lack of selection of international monies has been growingly apparent. Since the OPEC quadrupling of the oil price in 1973 OPEC governments have had huge reserves to invest. Their choice of liquid assets has been limited effectively to US dollars, West German marks and Swiss francs. Restrictions already described have narrowed the available investment forms of deutschmarks and Swiss francs. Both the German and Swiss governments have been concerned about the potential effect on their exchange rates of OPEC vagaries. The existence of a fourth independently floating international money – gold – would have deflected some of the weight of OPEC currency demand from the franc and mark.

LDCs would have had an alternative standard in which to denominate their debts. In practice LDCs have borrowed almost entirely in US dollars. By 1977, when the US was again running a large trade deficit and the dollar was under pressure, a switch of LDC borrowing toward gold would have been stabilising. The sale of borrowed dollars by LDCs in exchange for other currencies in order to make import payments was an added source of downward pressure on the dollar.

US TRADE DEFICITS

The US is a giant in the world economy. The dollar's role as an international money provides a shock absorber between shifts in the US balance of payments and the rest of the world.

A large US trade deficit is an expression of a desire by US residents to consume more than their production. The counterpart of their excess consumption must be a net accumulation of dollar-denominated assets by the rest of the world. If large international dollar credit markets in which many of the non-US participants were 'dollar dreamers' did not exist, the US trade supply of dollars would have to be absorbed wholly by currency speculators. Given the huge size of the US economy, the volume of dollar inventories to be absorbed could be large relative to what speculators have to cope with in other smaller currencies. Larger risk premiums would then have to be paid to entice the required extra marginal speculators to fulfil the task. The market mechanism of providing risk premiums – an extra immediate fall in the exchange rate followed by a steeper and more rapid climb to its eventual real level – could be disruptive to world trade.

Consider the $16 billion prospective US current account deficit in 1977. The flow of speculative funds to absorb dollars would come chiefly from three sources.

Firstly private speculators would borrow in the other two international credit markets denominated in the Swiss franc and deutschmark respectively. Some of the US deficit is likely to be reflected in German and Swiss trade surpluses, both being symptomatic of declining competitiveness of US exports. Speculators would short-sell deutschmarks and Swiss francs to buy dollars to the extent that the Swiss and German trade surpluses could be so explained by the US deficit. They realise that the adjustment of trade patterns to changed exchange rates occurs slowly. Sufficient deutschmark and Swiss franc appreciation against the dollar happens to promise speculators an eventual excess flow of francs and deutschmarks with which to repay their loans and earn a risk premium. The flow would be generated via a US basic surplus and a German and Swiss basic deficit once export industries in each country had had time to respond to the changed exchange rates.

Secondly some non-US investors may be so tempted by the speculative opportunity of buying dollars that they increase their savings. Their countries' trade surpluses are thus increased.

Thirdly central banks themselves will speculate. Countries with restricted currencies will also find their trade balances tending to swing into surplus. Their residents cannot speculate freely and so the central bank mops up some dollars in exchange for its own currency to prevent effecting a sharp appreciation. Some upward adjustment is probable even for restricted currencies because their issuers try to avoid making losses on their dollar purchases.

Fortunately large international dollar credit markets exist. The demand for dollar credit corresponding to the US trade deficit tends to push up dollar interest rates both in the euro-dollar and domestic US markets. Some non-US dreamers in dollars (including many Treasuries and central banks) are 'crowded out' of the dollar credit markets by the higher rates; others are tempted to increase their dollar asset holdings. Both reactions imply increased net savings by non-US residents who are lending effectively to finance part of the US deficit. The dollar's wide use as an international standard of value (dream quality) allows the US to finance part of the trade deficit by borrowing in its own currency. The cost of paying a currency risk premium to speculators is avoided. Residents of the metropolitan dollar area, the US, borrow from the greater dollar area which includes dollar dreamers all over the world. The euro-dollar market is a very rough proxy of the greater dollar area as it includes a high proportion of non-resident positions. It is impossible though to separate statistically dollar dreamers from dollar speculators.

Not all the US trade deficit is financed by borrowing from the greater dollar area. To tempt sufficient lenders there dollar interest rates would have to rise far above the domestic US market equilibrium level. The tendency of interest rates to rise in the euro-dollar market (the greater dollar area proxy) would be swamped by arbitrage flows from the much larger US market. Instead a proportion of the trade deficit is mopped up by speculators and a downward exchange rate adjustment occurs.

The relative proportion of the deficit absorbed by speculators and the greater dollar area is a function of the size of the euro- relative to the domestic currency credit market. If the euro-dollar market was much larger, the dollar exchange rate adjustment to a trade deficit would be smaller.

The Swiss franc is the world's most externalised currency. The size of the euro-franc deposit market is about equal to the Swiss money supply. The prospective trade deficit of Switzerland is of little significance to the determination of the franc's exchanging rate. Not much interest rate adjustment need occur for sufficient francs to be lent mainly by the commonwealth of franc dreamers outside Switzerland. The trade balance can be expected to be tiny compared to the total franc credit market.

IS DOLLAR MIGHT RIGHT?

The euro-dollar markets form an atmosphere round the non-American world through which the impact on other markets of dollar flows from the US is filtered. The US gains from the atmosphere being composed of dollars. Financing trade deficits is cheaper as less risk premium is payable.

The role of the euro-dollar market implies a special responsibility for the US Federal Reserve. If its monetary management deteriorated sharply, and the dollar became a volatile unit of account, the size of the euro-dollar market would shrink. Investors and borrowers would seek denomination in Swiss francs and deutschmarks. Atmospheric protection would become thin as a larger proportion of US capital and trade flows had to be absorbed by speculators.

The re-monetisation of gold in the form suggested earlier would not eliminate non-American dependence on Federal Reserve sobriety. Some international role for the dollar is essential to the smooth absorption of US balance of payments flows. Yet gold money is unique in not being a creature of a national political authority. The high-powered money of a paper gold system would be physical gold stocks which are distributed far and wide through every land.

6 Metamorphosis

The drama surrounding changing form has fascinated writers in all ages. Homer describes the terrible adventures of Ulysses' sailors in the palace of the enchantress Circe. By her exercise of magic she turns the sailors into pigs thus making their exterior conform to their hoggish disposition. Ulysses overpowers Circe and she promises to restore the sailors to human shape. When Ulysses is shown the swine in their sty he can see little difference between those that were hogs by birth and the twenty-two that were his sailors. Indeed the latter seemed to outdo the original swine in their own natural vocation. They wallowed in the dirtiest part of the sty.

The modern observer of the currency scene at end-1976 would readily have classed the pound with the Swedish kroner, Australian dollar, Italian lira and other currencies that are of restricted tradability and have little international usage. The modern pound and its management have few traces of their former selves. At the beginning of the twentieth century the pound was the major international money and the Bank of England 'could almost have claimed to be the conductor of the international orchestra' (Keynes). Today the UK authorities wallow unashamedly in the use of the tools of soft money management – exchange restrictions, protectionism, bear squeezes and bank deposit quotas.

The soft money form was confirmed on the pound during its summer crisis of 1976. For years, the British had eschewed the policies and constitutional limits of hard money managers, emulating instead those of soft. The international investment and trade use of the pound was slow to die. Finally UK economic management became embarrassed by the pound's outward form continuing to reflect shades of previous greater history. In December 1976 official enactments attempted to smother the pound's remaining international role. The pound's use in international trade finance was prohibited and steps were taken to discourage the use of pound denomination in UK foreign trade.

When Circe's wand turned Ulysses' sailors back into humans

their first reaction included a mingling of regrets. Forgetting their new shape they scramble to eat acorns. North Sea oil may be the wand that will transform the pound back into a hard money. Even so many years may pass before the pound's managers lose their soft money instincts.

Not all currency metamorphoses have been outward stamps of a changed motivation of the monetary authority. Some can be the result of deep political trauma. The descent of the German money into hyperinflation following the First World War was due at least in part to Germany's loss of large blocs of territory and the imposition of reparations obligations. Both measures led to huge sales of paper marks in the foreign exchange by the Government and ex-residents of Germany.

It is often the process of metamorphosis rather than the metamorphosed that fascinates us. We are interested in the decline and fall of the Roman Empire not primarily to gain an insight about modern Italy, but about a process that could recur with modern empires. Sterling's fall from its pre-eminent status in the world's currency markets is interesting as an example of money transformation rather than as an insight into the modern British pound and its future.

MARKETING MONEY

> Be not afraid of greatness: some men are born great, some
> achieve greatness, and some have greatness thrust upon them.
> Twelfth Night, Shakespeare.

In the aftermath of the Second World War, the US dollar was indisputably first among currencies. Not only was it the only major trading currency to be fully convertible, but non-resident holders were guaranteed exchangability into gold at a fixed rate. The US share of world trade had increased enormously. The international role of the dollar was thrust on it by the sheer weight of the US in the world economy and its relatively unimpaired state.

FIAT AND GOLD DOLLARS

There were in effect two US dollars in the period to August 1971.

The 'paper gold dollar' was held by non-US residents. They had the right – limited in 1968 – to demand physical gold at a fixed rate for dollars. So long as they were prepared to hold dollars rather than physical gold interest could be earned. The convenience rent on the metal equalled the dollar interest rate. The 'fiat dollar' was held only by US residents. They were barred legally from investing or trading in gold. When a US resident transferred fiat dollars to a non-resident they became paper gold dollars.

US Treasury and Federal Reserve gold operations ensured that the two types of dollar always traded at par. A private non-US resident wishing to convert his dollar deposit into gold would withdraw Federal Reserve (high-powered) money from his bank and convert it into gold at the Treasury.

In 1968 the US – with international agreement – re-labelled paper gold dollars held by private non-residents as fiat dollars. In future paper gold dollars could be held only by governmental institutions. Those gold dollars were phoney. The gold into which they were convertible could be sold only at the official price, far below the free market value of gold. That was the essence of the two-tier gold market from 1968 – 71. Ultimately, in August 1971, the remaining gold dollars were exchanged mandatorily at par into fiat dollars.

The decision to eliminate the paper gold dollar was not inevitable. In August 1971 the US could have instead revalued the gold dollar and allowed it to float freely against the fiat dollar. The fiction of an official gold price would have been ended summarily. The system so created would have resembled that described in Chapter 5 where gold (and paper gold) would have been an independent international money.

Technically the US would have decreed in August 1971 that a gold dollar was not worth say 0·020 ozs of gold instead of the previous rate of 0·029. The revaluation would have increased the ratio of physical gold stocks to gold dollars outstanding. The risk of gold cornering which had become acute would have so been reduced.

Private non-residents and residents would have been permitted to hold gold dollars. All physical gold, whether held by official institutions or private individuals, would have become salable in the free market. The US Treasury (or Federal Reserve) would have set an interest rate on gold dollars, at a level to balance supply and demand. Eventually the rate could have become determined freely by arbitrage between the gold futures dollar money and gold dollar markets. Other countries would have chosen whether to peg their currencies to the paper gold dollar, the fiat dollar or to float. Some foreign governments may have themselves started to issue their own brands of paper gold. Inter-governmental contracts would have been denominated sometimes in gold.

IMITATION DOLLARS

Between 1949 and 1967 sterling was pegged to the US dollar at a central rate of $2·80. Fluctuations were permitted up to one per cent in either direction from $2·80. The pound was effectively an imitation dollar. Its exchange rate against other currencies mirrored movements of the dollar. The pound did not carry a gold guarantee, but after 1957 convertibility into foreign currency was assured for non-residents.

Interest rates on pounds were typically greater than on dollars. The imitation dollar bills and bonds could therefore be sought for less than those denominated genuinely in dollars. The buyer of the imitation product ran the risk that it would deteriorate sooner – that its gold value would be adjusted down earlier.

The pound was an inferior product to the US dollar in other respects. It was issued behind walls of protection. UK exchange restrictions, first introduced as an emergency measure in 1939, became a permanency. After 1957 restrictions continued but applied only to residents. Sterling thus lacked the free tradability that was shown in Chapter 1 to be a necessary condition of international popularity.

'SOME MEN ARE BORN GREAT'

In 1945 the pound was second currency to the dollar. It was used widely to denominate international trade and finance. Businessmen are slow to change their pattern of currency denomination and investors are slow to change the currency of their dreams. Sterling had a head-start against all other currencies, save the dollar, in re-establishing firmly its international role after the war. A long reputation of sound management and a receptive market would have been the foundations. The post-war generation of sterling's managers was born into greatness.

A positive marketing strategy for sterling would have had to include a realistic appraisal of the UK's changed status in the world economy. The UK's dwindling share of world trade was likely in itself to lead to a declining international usage of the pound. That would have had to be offset in two ways. Firstly excellence of monetary management would have been developed. Secondly the promotion and innovation of investment instruments and loan facilities not available in other currencies would have been necessary.

Excellent monetary management should not have been interpreted as tying the pound to the dollar and becoming a shoddy imitation. Britain's post-war social and industrial evolution was likely to require some sharp real exchange rate changes. They would reflect altered relative productivity in traded and non-traded goods sectors and a changed pattern of UK foreign investment and income flows. Real exchange rate changes can be effected either by the nominal exchange rate or the internal price level. The latter method was clearly difficult given the highly monopolised labour markets in Britain. The conclusion would have been to allow the exchange rate to be freely determined in the market. Sterling would float.

Floating would not have solved by itself the problem of constructing a monetary policy likely to promote international usage of the pound. Investors and borrowers prefer a reliable, steady unit of account. Whilst recognising the UK's higher propensity to inflation the monetary authorities would have stressed predictability of the rate. Overshooting of a 3 – 4 per cent target would have been resisted. Interest rates would have had to be allowed to find their level in a free market, reflecting the pound's expected tendency to depreciate against the dollar. Exchange restrictions, credit rationing and other controls that tended to keep pound interest rates at an artificial level would have been abandoned.

Product differentiation is the name of the currency game. Investors in the floating pound would have added an independent component to their portfolios rather than a high risk dollar. The promoters of sterling would have infringed the fixed exchange rate provisions of the Bretton Woods code and have jeopardised the UK's access to IMF finance. It has been argued already in Chapter

4 that a freely floating hard currency is unlikely to require IMF assistance for stability.

Innovation of investment and loan forms is not initiated in governmental agencies. Official measures can though produce a framework within which their development is unlikely. Totally free convertibility would have been essential to innovation in the international use of the pound. Then a foreign pound bond market and commodity and currency futures markets using the pound as their vehicle currency could have been developed unimpeded. The promotion of the pound's international use would not have necessitated large capital drains from the UK. Foreign lenders, as much as borrowers, could have been tempted to use pound denomination by its independent unit of account feature and London's range of investment instruments. Recognised financial expertise in London would have led the world in market-making, much of its activity being in pounds.

Although sterling's managers were born into greatness their inheritance of past custom and goodwill could dwindle fast. Continued greatness would have had to be achieved in the ways suggested. But no committee met to market sterling. It was decided that the game was not worth the candle. The political economy arguments for and against that decision are not within the scope of this book. The pound is of interest here as a case-study in currency metamorphosis.

SOFT MONEY POLICIES

UK economic policy-makers adopted the language and tools of soft money managers long before the pound had become a localised currency with little international investment or trade appeal although with continuing speculative appeal. British officials were preoccupied with 'balance of payments', 'public sector borrowing' and 'bank lending' problems.

WHO COUNTS?

Very rich men do not know their wealth. Not only would its market value be hard to establish at any moment in time, but the whole exercise of counting would not be worthwhile. And so it is with currencies. Managers of small and/or restricted currencies must concern themselves with balance of payments problems. Exchange restrictions impede the efficient functioning of the speculative mechanism as illustrated in Chapter 4 and the central bank must assume a speculative role described as 'official financing'. Small currencies are often tied to larger ones so as to reduce dealing costs and exchange and interest rate volatility. Their managers are concerned with balance of payments developments in order to adjust monetary policy to ensure feasibility of a continued fixed exchange rate.

The issuers of a money used internationally need not pay close attention to their state's balance of payments. The Swiss National Bank is not much concerned whether Switzerland will this year run a trade deficit and what the size of that deficit will be. The large commonwealth of Swiss franc users outside Switzerland absorb readily such trade flows with minor franc interest rate or exchange rate adjustment. The US Treasury and Federal Reserve is not perturbed by forecasts of trade or capital account deficits. They can rely on the resilience of the euro-dollar markets and depth of speculative interest in the dollar to absorb dollars flows from the US economy.

British policy-makers' worries throughout the 1950s and 60s about how to 'balance' the international accounts foreshadowed the shrunken pound status of the mid-70s rather than its then potential. The more grandiose policy option of promoting the pound's internationalisation would have ensured that the British did not one day have to stoop to a preoccupation with balancing their international payments.

THE LANDMARK THAT WAS NOT

In June 1972 the pound was floated. The break from the dollar marked neither a late initiative to market the pound positively as an independent currency nor to restore free tradability. New measures were introduced simultaneously to shrink the sterling area to include only the British Isles and Gibraltar.

By 1973 it had become clear that the float was very mirky. Not only was day to day intervention sizable, but a programme of massive quasi-intervention was activated under the title of the 'local authority and nationalised industries exchange cover scheme'.

Instead of borrowing foreign currency under its own name the UK
government directed public sector agencies to do so and they would
be reimbursed for losses resulting from exchange rate fluctuations.
The uncertain timing and amounts of quasi-official exchange
market intervention added to the hazards of investing or otherwise
dealing in the pound.

Governments of states that issue international monies – the US,
West Germany and Switzerland – do not borrow in foreign currencies nor in foreign capital markets. Foreign exchange market
intervention, in so far as it occurs, is the exclusive responsibility of
the central bank. International lines of credit are established in its
own name. Sometimes governmental agencies will borrow foreign
currency because their treasurers believe that financing costs will be
reduced thereby. They stake their borrowing strategy on a
particular exchange rate view. The central government does not
promise compensation for erroneous judgment.

The Canadian dollar is freely tradable and has floated freely for
much of the post-war period. The Canadian government borrows
exclusively in the Canadian capital market. Provincial and city
governments on the other hand have been frequent users of the New
York and euro-bond markets. Some provinces, particularly Manitoba, have tried to use speculative judgment to their advantage.
Manitoba has borrowed mixed bags of yen, deutschmarks, US
dollars and Hong Kong dollars. Its selection of currencies has no
more to do with official exchange market policy than the borrowing
practices of Ford Canada Ltd.

SPECULATION IN MANIPULATED CURRENCIES

Buyers of seats at Lloyds – the world-famous London insurance
underwriters – are gamblers. They must deposit a stake of £80,000
(approximately). They expect to make a good return from their
share of premium income. But they face unlimited loss. If there is a
major disaster, their personal property to its full extent can be sold
to meet claims. The Lloyds' member is willing to accept the minute
risk of absolute ruin to earn a normally excellent return.

The counterpart of the Lloyds' member in the foreign exchange
market invests in heavily manipulated currencies. Interventionist
central banks tend to peg their exchange rates for long periods of
time. Intermittent free floats happen during which large rate

movements occur. The intermissions of floating are very short compared to the periods of stability. If intervention is designed to postpone depreciation, interest rates remain higher than on the currency being used as a peg. When the pound was stabilised against the dollar, in the years of UK trade deficit 1973–6, UK interest rates remained higher than dollar ones, often by a considerable margin.

The Lloyds' member currency market counterpart in 1976 would have bought pounds during times of stability, hoping to make an exit before the next floating intermission. Sometimes his timing would be wrong and he would record a large loss. His operations would not be confined to pounds. Running returns of 30–40 per cent per annum could have been made by taking long positions in Spanish pesetas, Italian lire and Mexican pesos for much of 1976–7. It was essential to avoid the short intervals of plummeting depreciations!

The extraordinary speculative profits in the currency game are made by a different type of risk-bearer. He speculates in the opposite direction to the central bank. During a period of capital flight or trade deficit, when the central bank persists in absorbing excess supplies of currencies at the pegged rate, he *short-sells* the currency. He believes that the central bank is paying too high a price for its currency and that reserve losses will enforce a reduction. He acts as a first-order speculator, short-selling currency to meet what he believes is an artificial shortage created by extravagant central bank demand. Eventually the central bank pulls the plugs out and allows the exchange rate to 'find its own level'. His purchase of currency at that date to close his short position helps stabilise the market in the aftermath of the sudden cessation of central bank demand.

Profit-taking by fortunate speculators is a familiar feature of the freely-floating intermissions. Their purchase of currency helps absorb continuing excess supplies without the exchange rate having to fall so low as to tempt in new first-order speculators. The old ones are realizing certain profits when they purchase the currency without assuming a risky position.

Exchange rate manipulation by the British authorities led to perverse speculation in the first half of 1977, but in the opposite direction to usual. A net investment and trade demand developed for the pound as the current account moved into surplus and the UK equity and bond markets attracted foreign purchasers. The Bank of England sold pounds at a rate of near $1·71, satisfying excess demand. Many speculators believed that the authorities would eventually try to reap political advantage from allowing the rate to float up rather than ease restrictions on capital outflows. Those speculators purchased pounds believing the large official supply of them in the market to be transient. They acted as first-order speculators.

In the mirky floating years following 1972 the pound was a currency well-suited to 'perverse' speculation. The combination of low transaction costs, and long periods of becalmed markets, offered strong temptation.

BANANA REPUBLIC TREATMENT

There was much-voiced opposition both in the popular and financial media to IMF terms imposed on the UK in 1967 and again in 1976. A frequent complaint was that the list of conditions was of the same nature as that applied normally to the IMF's LDC clients. The similarity was not coincidental, but the result of the policy selection of a restricted currency role for the pound rather than an international one. The contention can be illustrated by the IMF's limiting of the size of the UK's public sector borrowing requirement (PSBR).

Assuming that a money supply target is set independently the importance of the PSBR is its effect on the level of private investment activity. The issue of public debt might decrease significantly the total of funds available for private investment. That would concern the IMF, in the role of lender, if it was believed that investment was required in the export sector to sustain a trade surplus sufficient to restore external account strength.

Where domestic currency is freely tradable and has international investment appeal the opportunity cost of a given PSBR is less. The more internationalised the bond market in the local currency, the smaller will be the interest rate rise caused by government demand for funds. The US PSBR must be compared for example not with the size of the domestic US credit market, but with the domestic and international dollar markets combined. If the government debt issue puts upward pressure on local interest rates, investors will tend to switch into the local capital market from foreign securities. Free currency tradability ensures that the expected domestic real rate of return should tend to equal that on other hard money investments.

Speculative inflows in response to higher interest rates reduce the real domestic oportunity cost of the PSBR. Official preoccupation with the UK's PSBR was a symptom of the pound's metamorphosis.

SOFT CREDIT COMPETITION

In the summer of 1971 the Bank of England launched a new domestic credit policy under the banner of 'Competition and Credit Control'. The idea was to eliminate official directives on bank sterling lending policy and permit open competition between banks in their sterling liability management. The new era was short-lived. By December 1973 a new system of quotas was applied to banks. Ceilings were set to the growth of deposit liabilities for each bank. Rather than using the tool of high-powered money control, official preference was shown for detailed limits whose effect was to impede bank competition.

Quota control would be an instrument ill-suited for money management by central banks of international investment currencies. Application would lead to a rapid loss of custom by domestic banks to foreign competitors. If a wide euro-pound market existed, to which UK residents had free access, many would switch their deposit and loan business to there. They would thus escape the rigours of domestic controls.

STERLING EXODUS 1976

A remarkable change in investment sentiment both towards the pound and the UK occurred in the Spring of 1976. Large non-resident holders of sterling decided to reduce or eliminate it as one of the permanent components of their portfolio. The change in currency tastes can be explained by a variety of developments. The pound had become volatile and the competence of the sterling monetary authorities was questioned widely. There was a growing realisation that the restricted tradability of the pound would prevent pound interest rates from rising to a level sufficient to provide a risk premium for the greater volatility of sterling than dollars, Swiss francs and deutschmarks. Official holders of the pound, who were concentrated in OPEC, reduced their pound investments by £1·5 bn during 1976.

The outflow of pounds revealed by balance of payments statistics is an *ex post* measure. The discrepancy between intended and realized capital outflows is absorbed by speculators (public or private). Statistics do not show how much sterling was sold by previous long-run investors to speculators. The latter would mop up excess pounds at an exchange rate believed to be sufficiently low to generate over a longer period a trade surplus of similar size.

Balance of payments statistics reveal the amount of speculation by the public sector. In 1976 UK authorities mopped up over $8 bn worth of pounds. The purchases were from three sources. Firstly some of the pounds sold by investors deciding to eliminate sterling from their portfolios were doubtless bought. Secondly the UK continued to run a sizable trade deficit in 1976, creating a further net supply of pounds to be absorbed by speculators, private or public. Thirdly official intervention tactics involved stabilising the exchange rate for several weeks and then withdrawing altogether from the market. In consequence first-order private speculators tended to operate in the opposite direction to fundamental currency flows. They would short-sell pounds, believing that the Bank of England was stabilising the exchange rate 'at too high a level', and that the official net demand for pounds at that rate would be temporary. 'Too high a level' means at a higher rate than that at which private speculators would be prepared to absorb excess pounds given their calculation about the depreciation required to generate an equal trade surplus.

HISTORICAL PRECEDENTS

The operation of speculators in a currency subject to large withdrawals can be illustrated colourfully by the German experience after the First World War. According to the Ultimatum of London of May 1921 Germany had to pay 1 billion gold marks of reparations by end-August and a further 500 million by November. Bresciani-Turroni records that half the first sum was obtained by the Reichsbank selling paper marks in the foreign exchange market. Panic spread and in one month the rate slid from 241·1/$ to 422·4/$. The crisis was exacerbated when the decision of the Council of the League of Nations relating to the division of Upper Silesia became known. The consequences of the loss of territory were feared to be a decrease of net export revenues and a flood of further marks from now ex-residents of Germany onto the market.

Speculators were attacked sometimes vehemently in the German press for causing the collapse of the market in the foreign exchanges. In reality if net speculative demand had not absorbed the glut of paper marks, the collapse would have been even greater. Speculators were too optimistic in their calculation. The celebrated McKenna Report estimated the profit received by Germany from the sale of marks to non-resident speculators to be three times that paid in foreign exchange on account of reparations.

The payment of reparations imposes a tax on domestic residents. If the government does not itself run a budget surplus equal to the reparation obligation, the tax is collected implicitly. The exchange rate fall caused by the government sale of paper in the foreign exchange market inflicts a loss on holders of government debt, including money. The loss represents revenue essentially equivalent to the well-known inflation tax on money.

FUNDING

By Autumn 1976 officials had become aware that the pound crisis was now rooted in a feared mass withdrawal of capital from the UK. Schemes were discussed for 'funding' the sterling balances. Each plan had as its objective the lengthening of the period over which the trade surplus equal to the intended capital withdrawal would be generated. Rather than depending on risk-averse speculators to absorb temporarily the sterling sold by its present holders, would there not be a social gain from an intergovernmental arrangement whereby the sterling was mopped up and then disposed of over a much longer time-span? The premise of any funding operation was that the stage had now been reached where irreparable damage had been done to sterling as an international currency and all that remained to be done was to cooperate with those evacuating the sterling market in order to reduce adjustment costs.

The essence of funding was to complete 'off-the-market' deals with large official holders of sterling. In the Basel agreement of January 1977 the UK authorities agreed to offer long-term foreign currency bonds to official holders in exchange for their sterling. That would allow the UK a much longer time over which to accommodate the reduction of pound investments than if they were absorbed by private speculators. The plan was potentially expensive. Official holders were able to liquidate their pound balances at a higher exchange rate than if sold collectively in the open market.

The offer of foreign currency bonds in April 1977 was historically a non-event. The take-up amounted to £394 m., or a little less than a fifth of the outstanding £2·2 bn of official balances. Sterling prospects had improved following the acceptance of the IMF loan conditions in December 1976 and the emerging UK trade surplus due to North Sea oil.

INTERNATIONAL ROLE ATTACKED

Funding was not the exclusive official response to the 1976 sterling crisis. In December 1976 a new protectionist package of exchange restrictions was introduced. The longer-term aim was the elimination of the pound's remaining international role. UK residents were now prohibited from extending pound loans to finance trade between third countries. In consequence the pound was unlikely to be used as a currency denominator in international trade. It was demonstrated in Chapter 5 how international availability of trade finance in the currency was essential to that role. Within weeks of the new decree the minor metal trades had switched their unit of denomination from pounds to dollars.

Steps were taken simultaneously to encourage UK exporters to switch to dollar financing. Subsidised export credit was made available in dollars. The effect was to reduce pound loans to non-residents and cause a once for all capital inflow equal to net repayment.

The changing pattern of trade finance would have been of less consequence if the pound had been a freely tradable currency. The reduction of short-term pound trade loans to non-residents would have tended to be matched by a reduction of forward pound purchases. Many international traders hedge their pound loans by buying pounds forward. The simultaneous purchase of spot pounds to repay domestic pound trade loans and decrease in demand for forward pounds have an identical exchange rate effect to borrowing euro-pounds to lend pounds in the UK. If arbitrage was permitted freely between the euro- and domestic pound market, reducing the pound's trade financing role would have had little effect on the pound exchange rate. Flows between the euro- and domestic market of a freely tradable currency do not influence its exchange rate. The official encouragement of non-pound trade financing belonged to the soft money policy instrument kit.

CURRENCY AND COMMODITY AUCTIONS

A striking feature of UK official exchange intervention policy since the floating of the pound in 1972 has been its volatility. Massive intervention in one month could be followed by one in which the authorities were inactive. The source of volatility has been the emphasis on target exchange rate levels.

The setting of target exchange rates for the pound led to huge perverse speculative flows. The official judgment of appropriate rates was widely questioned by market operators. Instead of the monetary authorities and private speculators operating net in the same direction they often partially offset each other.

INTERVENTION RATIONALE?

Intervention, sometimes on a massive scale, by the UK authorities has been grounded in concern about the private speculative function. In 1976 officials feared that, if the Bank of England had withdrawn altogether from the market, the exchange rate would have plummeted. They would not have denied that, if the rate had fallen sufficiently, speculators would have mopped up the excess pounds. They believed however that given the scale of capital outflows to be absorbed the risk premium required by speculators would be very large. The exchange rate would have had to overshoot by a wide margin the level required to generate a trade surplus equal to the intended capital withdrawal. The margin represents the reward to the speculator for assuming risk. Further risk-averse speculators wish to realize profits quickly. The exchange rate would have fallen to a level that would have generated a large trade surplus in a short time rather than a smaller running surplus over a longer period.

The risk arguments for official interventions are particularly relevant to currencies without international investment appeal. Countries that issue an international money do not face the problem of rapid forced adjustment to developments in their balance of payments. Part of the adjustment is shouldered by borrowing (or lending) from the external markets in their currency. Only that proportion of flows absorbed by speculators has a direct impact on the exchange rate. Speculation is more competitive in international monies and risk premiums expected are less. The monies have a reputation of stability and information relevant to speculative judgment is readily available. International bond markets are denominated mainly in hard monies and the bonds' bearer and tax-exempt qualities attract the longer-term speculator. Long-term speculation is often not possible in soft monies because of the lack of suitable instruments.

In sum an argument for official intervention in soft currencies – those without investment appeal – is the comparative weakness of the speculative function there. Is it not reasonable that at least a similar proportion of currency flows should be officially absorbed for soft monies as are absorbed by external markets in hard monies?

The above defence for soft money exchange intervention does not justify the official setting of exchange rate targets. At no point has the argument appealed to the superior speculative judgment of governmental agencies. Appeal has been made to the official capacity to absorb excess soft currency inventories over a longer period of time and for less risk reward than private speculators. The operational guidelines for the official intervention agency should be expressed simply in terms of target levels of currency purchases (or sales). The exchange rate is determined by competition between private speculators who take account of announced official intervention targets.

The setting of targets would take a similar form to that of money supply targets. Each quarter the authorities would announce target weekly sales (or purchases) for up to one year ahead. The targets would be revised at the end of each quarter in the light of changing economic developments. Within each week the sales (or purchases) would occur daily in equal amounts and at a stated time.

Suppose the method of intervention was applied to sterling. Participants would know that the Bank of England was in the market daily to sell, say $20 million at midday. The Bank's main clients would be probably commercial traders hoping to save transaction costs of dealing with brokers and market-makers. Suppose the going market quote for pounds was 1·6805–15. The commercial customer would hope to buy dollars from the Bank at around $1·6810/£. Both he and the Bank would gain from bypassing the market-maker. An informal auction would in effect be conducted by the Bank.

1976–7 REVISITED

The overwhelming impression from a study of sterling intervention policy is one of short-sightedness. An arbitrary exchange rate would be 'pulled out of a hat' and defended against speculative attacks in either direction. The speculator is likely to be the official's enemy in such a system. If instead quantity targets had been set, speculators must almost inevitably be operating net in the same direction as officials.

Suppose a quantity target intervention system had been operated. At end-December 1975 a balance of trade deficit was forecast for 1976; there was no reason to predict a sudden exodus from the pound. Official dollar sales equal to say 50 per cent of the current account deficit would have been announced for 1976. At end-March 1976 a revised target would have been announced for intervention until March 1977. Suspicions of intended pound withdrawals were already widespread and the intervention target for the immediate quarter March to June 1976 would have been increased over the prospective level set in December 1975.

By December 1976 forecasts were widespread of a narrower UK current account deficit in 1977. The authorities were also aware that their exchange restrictions on the use of the pound in trade finance would cause a capital inflow of up to $1·5 billion within the first half of 1977. They could therefore have announced a target sale of £1 billion for 1977 all to be effected in the first half. The inflow together with the IMF facility would have restored the official reserves to a more normal level. The huge perverse speculative inflows that occurred in expectation of the pound being allowed to float above its arbitrarily chosen peg of $1·71 would have been avoided.

COPPER MARKET INTERVENTION

The principle of intervention by setting quantity targets can be illustrated further in analysis of commodity buffer stock operations. The example of copper is used. By mid-1977 copper inventories were 1·5 million tons above their normal level related to world consumption. The free market price had fallen to 52 ¢s per pound. Copper industry studies showed that the price would have to rise to $1·00 per pound to justify new mine development. Excess world inventories were held by speculators who believed that within several years the metal's price must have risen to equal the replacement cost.

Advocates of a buffer stock for copper argued that investment interest in the metal was not widespread. The price had fallen ridiculously low to tempt sufficient speculators to hold the huge surplus inventories. The marginal speculators required very high risk premiums and wanted to see a quick profit. The danger of continued low prices was that by the mid-1980s an acute shortage of copper may have resulted from the present lack of incentive to invest in the copper industry.

A buffer stock would operate with a longer-time horizon than many private speculators and expect less risk return. The buffer stock manager (BSM) would operate by buying say 4000 tons of copper daily for 100 days. 400,000 tons would so be transferred from private speculators to the BSM. The copper price would rise for two reasons. Firstly the marginal speculators who required the highest risk premiums would have withdrawn selling their copper to the BSM. Secondly remaining private speculators would know that the BSM would not intend to off-load its inventory until copper shortages were again prevalent.

The BSM would buy copper in similar fashion to the Bank of England buying pounds. At noon his agent on the floor of the London Metal Exchange (LME) would invite tenders for copper. Suppose the bid-offer spread is £680–1 per ton spot. Commercial sellers would offer him copper at £680½. Both would gain from the elimination of the market-maker spread. During periods of metal shortage the BSM would announce a programme of copper sales of equal daily amount. An informal auction would take place daily on the LME.

PERVERSE SPECULATION IN TIN

The pitfalls of target price intervention can be demonstrated to be similar in commodities and in currencies. The International Tin Agreements have long provided for buffer stock intervention. The BSM's guidelines are expressed in price ranges. A floor and ceiling price are set periodically. The BSM must sell tin to prevent the tin price breaking through the ceiling: he buys tin to prevent the price falling through the floor. Within a middle price range intervention is discretionary.

Historically the BSM has been more successful at defending the floor than the ceiling. The size of the BSM's inventory limits his power to counter price surges. When the price nears the ceiling, and the BSM's inventory is believed to be low, many speculators buy tin in anticipation of a free float of tin. The speculation is first-order in nature based on the belief that the BSM's supply is temporary. The direction of speculation is counter to economic fundamentals. Given the excess of industrial consumption over production of tin, speculators should be net sellers to commercial users of the metal. The present method of operation of the BSM creates large flows of metal between two groups of speculators – official sellers and private buyers.

CURRENCY EVOLUTION

The benefits of floating exchange rates had long been debated before the collapse of the Bretton Woods edifice of fixed rates in August 1971. It was little realised that the success of a free float would depend crucially on sophistication of both monetary authorities and financial market organisation. The essential role of the private speculator has been highlighted at many stages in this book. Low-cost speculation – readiness to absorb excess currency supplies and conversely for low-risk rewards – is possible only in hard monies. They are traded actively, not subject to great uncertainty, and denominate a wide selection of investment instruments that have an international appeal.

Joining a freely floating exchange rate system is a serious option only for monetary authorities of hard monies. They are few. The process of turning a soft money into hard is long and is more difficult for small than large currencies. The special problems of small currency management have been emphasised here. Government will is not sufficient basis for currency metamorphosis from soft to hard. Relevant skills must exist in the financial community to make markets in which speculators can deal.

Any country, large or small, developed or undeveloped, was eligible for membership of the world's oldest international monetary system – gold. The Bretton Woods system was similarly indiscriminating. The greater part of the world will continue to peg or control the float of their currencies.

Some of the proponents of flexible exchange rates have argued that they permitted greater national independence in monetary affairs. Each state could choose in accordance with social and industrial structure the appropriate rate of inflation. Beyond that, isolationist policies undermine the workings of a free float. Preventing foreigners holding a currency, and insulating the domestic interest rates from international influences, make speculative adjustment to balance of payments disequilibria more painful.

The German historian Treitschke wrote: 'Eternal peace is not a dream but a nightmare. It will only be achieved when the ice penetrates the sun and the stars turned black and trackless, start from their orbit.' A freely floating exchange rate system represents the latest stage reached of international monetary development. It is inconceivable that the system will ever embrace all national monies. The metamorphosis of currencies, from hard to soft and soft to hard, will continue to be a source of periodic turmoil in the world's money markets. Gold, the one-time hardest money, is but the latest to change its identity.

Bibliography

R. Z. Aliber, *The International Money Game* (London: Macmillan, 1977).

R. Z. Aliber, 'Monetary Rules and Monetary Reform', in R. Z. Aliber (ed.), *The Political Economy of Monetary Reform* (London: Macmillan, 1977).

R. Z. Aliber, 'Attributes of National Monies and the Interdependence of National Monetary Policies', in R. Z. Aliber (ed.), *National Monetary Policies and the International Financial System* (Chicago: University of Chicago Press, 1974).

S. W. Black, 'International Money Markets and Flexible Exchange Rates', *Princeton Studies in International Finance, No. 32*, (1973).

B. D. Brown, 'The Forward Sterling Market and its Relation to Arbitrage between the Silver Market in London, Chicago, and New York', *Oxford Economic Papers*, 29 (1977) 292–311.

B. D. Brown, 'Exchange Restrictions: Their Implication for Portfolio Management', *Economic Journal*, 87 (1977), 543–53.

C. A. Coombs, *The Arena of International Finance* (John Wylie, 1976).

J. R. Dominguez, *Devaluation and Futures Markets* (Lexington Books, 1972).

R. Dornbusch, 'Devaluation, Money and Non-traded Goods', *American Economic Review*, 73 (1973), 871–80.

M. Friedman, 'In Defense of Destabilising Speculation', in M. Friedman, *The Optimum Quantity of Money* (London: Macmillan 1969).

T. A. Hieronymus, *Economics of Futures Trading* (Commodity Research Bureau Incorp., 1971).

W. McClam,   'Credit Substitution and Euro-Currency Market', *Quarterly Review*, Banca Nazionale del Lavoro, 133 (1972).

H. W. Mayer,   'Some Theoretical Problems Relating to the Euro-dollar Market' *Princeton Essays in International Finance*, no. 79 (1970).

L. G. Telser,   'Futures Trading and the Storage of Cotton and Wheat', *Journal of Political Economy*, 66 (1958) 233–55.

Index

Amsterdam, 34, 35, 36; banks, 38

Andorra, 46, 126

Arbitrage, between black and official markets, 7–8; between euro- and domestic dollars, 70–1, 135; between euro- and domestic pounds, 21, 168; between euro- and domestic Swiss francs, 140; between euro- and domestic yen, 142; between Federal funds and euro-dollars, 62–3, 135; between Frankfurt, LME, and Zurich, 79–80; between Luxembourg and Frankfurt, 61–2, 135; between Paris and New York gold market, 134; covered interest, 14, 48, 53, 100, 119; covered parity, 16, 69, 97; in copper, 67, 77; in paper gold, 147; triangular, 43

Associate market, defined, 35; Federal funds market, 136; guilder money market, 38; IMM and interbank market, 83

Australian dollar, 155; euro-failure in, 53; restrictions, 57

Bahrain, dinar, 64; Monetary Authority, 40, 64; riyal market in, 36, 143–4

Banana republic treatment, 164

Bank for International Settlements, 47

Bank of England, 91; currency auctions, 170–2; free lunch, 92; intervention, 163, 166; mercantilism, 129; short-sells pounds, 100; use of Bear Squeeze, 114–15

Bank of France, 150

Bank of Italy, 7

Bank of Japan, 131; nationalistic response, 142

Bank secrecy, 137

Bank vaults, 67; subterranean, 151

Banknotes, Basel market in, 8; bid-offer spreads in, 8–9; market-making in, 45

Basel, banknote market, 8

Bear, grizzly and koala, 115; in Chicago, 135; on dollar, 133; on Sterling, 98

Bear squeeze, in Berlin 1894, 114; use by Bank of England, 114–15

Bearer, 68, 171; commodity warrants, 67, 75, 79; dollar notes, 88; guilder bonds, 128, 139; Swiss equities, 139–40

Belgian franc, 17, 102–3, 121, 126; convertible and financier, 29; domestic money market in, 59; failure to excite investment interest in, 18; *see also* Euro-

Berlin, 114, 134

Bid-ask spreads, 17; in dual exchange markets, 18; in small currencies, 101

Black markets, 6; bid-offer spreads in, 8; in Czech croner, 6; in Italian lira, 7; in Sterling, 6; *see also* Parallel markets

Bond market, *see* Euro-, Foreign-, International-

Bourse, 101, 134

Bretton Woods, 24, 43, 122, 159, 173, 174

British pound, 75, 155; artificial shortage, 98; as imitation dollar, 159; as unit of account, 159; black market, 35–6; British paper gold, 150; convenience rent on, 98–9; crash, 99; foreign exchange market, 35–6; forward market in, 9; free market, 71; heady days, 21; in Frankfurt, 44; international role, 155; trading on IMM, 82; *see also* Euro-